Preparing the Bride of Christ For His Return

My Journey with God

JANET VAN HIERDEN

WESTBOW·
PRESS
A DIVISION OF THOMAS NELSON
& ZONDERVAN

Scriptures taken from the Holy Bible, New International Version®, NIV®. Copyright © 1973, 1978, 1984, 2011 by Biblica, Inc.™ Used by permission of Zondervan. All rights reserved worldwide. www.zondervan.com The "NIV" and "New International Version" are trademarks registered in the United States Patent and Trademark Office by Biblica, Inc.™

WestBow Press books may be ordered through booksellers or by contacting:

WestBow Press
A Division of Thomas Nelson & Zondervan
1663 Liberty Drive
Bloomington, IN 47403
www.westbowpress.com
1 (866) 928-1240

ISBN: 978-1-4908-1820-7 (sc)
ISBN: 978-1-4908-1821-4 (hc)
ISBN: 978-1-4908-1819-1 (e)

Library of Congress Control Number: 2013922044

Printed in the United States of America.

WestBow Press rev. date: 12/13/2013

Awaiting the King

Let us rejoice and be glad and give Him glory!
For the wedding of the Lamb has come, and His bride has
made herself ready.

Revelation 19:7

The Father of Glory is doing a magnificent work among His people,
His bride – making her holy, cleansing her by the washing with water
through the Word, presenting her to Himself as a radiant church,
without stain or wrinkle or any other blemish, but holy and blameless.

In this prophetic image the bride who has been made ready is standing
in a river, representing being baptized in the glory, awaiting the Lion
of Judah, King of Kings and Lord of Lords, standing in the doorway at
the end of the great hall.

And the Spirit and the bride say, Come. And let him that
heareth say, Come.
And let him that is athirst come. And whosoever will, let
him take the water of life freely.

Revelation 22:17

Contents

PART III:
Secrets of the Kingdom of Darkness Revealed

Foreword

by Graham Power

I was born and raised in Cape Town, South Africa in the Apartheid Years.

At the age of forty three—in February, 1999—I went on my knees late at night in my study and invited Christ to take control of my life 24/7 (24 hours a day, 7 days of the week). I handed my life, family, and business over to God.

Having grown up with limited finances and very little luxury in our lives, I spent my working career chasing success, and reached a point where I had no inner peace. I started my own Construction and Property Development Company in 1983 (a little more than 30 years ago) yet, regardless of the material wealth I gained there was no inner peace.

Sixteen months later God gave me a detailed vision/instruction through a dream at 4:00 a.m., to start the Global Day of Prayer by inviting Christians from all denominations to join together for 'a Day of Repentance and Prayer.' In 2001, 45,000 people from diverse cultural and racial backgrounds gathered at the Newlands Stadium in Cape Town. Since then, this 'God inspired Vision' has each year progressively 'rolled out' across Africa and the Globe.

In 2009 approximately 400 million Christians gathered in 220 nations, across the Globe on Pentecost Sunday.

It was during this exciting GDOP 'roll-out' that I had the privilege of meeting Janet and Peter Van Hierden in Canada in 2007.

They were part of the coordinating committee for the event in Lethbridge Alberta, and it was here that I came face to face with this dynamic couple. A year later, in 2008, they visited us in Cape Town and we spent quality time together. It was during that time, that I came to see Janet's prophetic and discerning talents from GOD.

As I have read and been engrossed through this exciting and amazing testimony of Janet and Peter's life experiences, I have been challenged, encouraged, and inspired.

The challenges we all encounter in our Christian walk; the battles, hurts and many mountains we need to climb, have all come alive as Janet takes us on a wonderfully detailed journey of life.

As I think of the scripture in Ephesians 4, that talks about 'maturity' and being tossed back and forth by the waves, I realize that each of us needs to go through these 'storms' and humbling experiences; before we truly mature in our faith.

Janet's teenage challenges, being a mother, a spouse, an intercessor and a friend to many, leaves one with admiration for her boldness and obedience.

She describes the depression, brokenness, suffering and rejection— which most, if not all, of us will experience—in such a passionate way!

Being faced with witchcraft; the Jezebel spirit, taking Spiritual authority and hearing the voice of God is so ably articulated, that even the 'new' Christian will be armed and equipped to identify and recognize these challenges when they arise.

The three stages of Christianity, from the recently committed 'Convenience' stage to the 'Crisis' stage and ultimately the 'Intimacy/Obedience' stage are so well described!

I worked through this manuscript with such peace of mind, being reminded that we all go through these challenges and 'seasons' in order to reach that spiritual maturity in Christ.

I thank God for Janet's life, for her willingness to share her emotions, humbling experiences and pitfalls. I pray that this great book will be placed in the hands of thousands of men and women across the globe so that each of us can be well equipped and armed for the experiences and challenges which The Lord and Satan may bring across our paths.

May God use this exciting Van Hierden Family Testimony to encourage and inspire each of us to grow into our full 'purpose and calling.'

I pray 2 Chronicles 7:14 over your life and family; that we will all "humble ourselves and pray, seek His face and turn from our wicked ways" and that GOD will "hear from Heaven, forgive our sins and heal our land" (beginning with each of you dear readers—that GOD will heal you personally and your families) and bring you great peace and joy in The Lord.

Graham Power
(Power Group|Global Day of Prayer|Unashamedly Ethical)

Introduction

"Thy grace and Thy glory I will publish abroad."

This book is about the grace the Lord gives each of us to be an overcomer, to empower us in our weakness: "My grace is sufficient for you, for my power is made perfect in weakness" (2 Cor. 12:9). Grace empowers us to do what truth demands of us. The power of God is activated grace, a grace that will advance the Kingdom call upon our lives. Through this we mature as the Bride of Christ. Only by the Holy Spirit within us are we able to endure to the end. As we walk with the Lord and in the light of His Word, filled with the Holy Spirit, we will overcome. "His divine power has given us everything we need for life and godliness . . ." (2 Peter 1:3a).

This book is also a testimony of "overcoming by the blood of the lamb," and how the grace of God has been manifested in my life in many ways. It is a journal of my walk with God and how the Lord has instructed me, led me, and surrounded me. May this encourage you to be the overcomer that God desires. This word of my testimony is what the Lord called me to publish to encourage His people to endure, to bring glory to His name, to release His glory on earth, and cover our land from sea to sea.

I wrote this book in obedience to the voice of the Lord. Without the compelling voice of God through the Holy Spirit I would not and could not, because I do not consider myself a writer.

Numerous people have commented in the last several years, "Janet, you need to write a book," or, "the Lord spoke to me that He has given you much revelation you must release to God's people." But words alone would not compel me to write.

My heart cried out to God, "Lord, please speak to me. If this suggestion is from You, make it abundantly clear to me." Then the Lord began to drop impressions in my spirit preparing me for the day I heard His voice with clarity.

On June 3, 2010 the Lord clearly spoke to me as my husband and I attended a wedding. During the worship, we sang the words, "Thy grace and Thy glory I will publish abroad." I felt such power with those words I knew the many prophecies I'd received about writing were truly of the Lord. Overwhelmed by these words, I wrote them down and placed them in my purse. One week later I found this paper and as I read again the words I had written, "Thy grace and Thy glory I will publish abroad," I felt the Holy Spirit overpower me. I felt as though thunder hit my chest, and I could only groan and weep before the Lord. The moment had come and I could not delay.

Over the years, the Lord has taught me obedience and I will not ignore His voice. When He speaks twice to confirm it, He speaks strongly, as Genesis 41:32: "The reason the dream was given to Pharaoh in two forms is that the matter has been firmly decided by God . . ." When the Lord speaks twice in Scripture, He wants to emphasize the importance of His message. By repeating: "verily, verily I say unto you," He warns us to take special notice of His words. He knows how overly cautious I am of moving forward if I am unsure.

Confirmation of God's call was a revelation of God's glory to me. God is releasing His glory on this earth. I saw the glory come down and felt the glory hit me like a heat seeking missile. I collapsed under the incredible power of God, weeping and groaning in His presence as I heard the words being spoken by our pastor: "YOU are approved of God, you ARE approved of God, you are APPROVED of God, you are approved of GOD, YOU ARE APPROVED OF GOD!"

I felt the love of God being released as Jesus did at His baptism, when God spoke from heaven, "This is My beloved Son of whom I am well pleased." As we walk forward by grace, which is the empowerment of the Holy Spirit, He enables us to be overcomers and we walk in obedience to His voice. This brings His glory upon us so we can release it to others, and His glory will cover our land.

On a later date I sat at the piano, and opened the songbook at random to "We've a Story to Tell to the Nations." I felt I was drowning in the presence of the Lord for over thirty minutes. This song went deep in my spirit and I knew I must tell you my story.

> We've a story to tell to the nations, that shall turn their hearts to the right,
> A story of truth and mercy, a story of peace and light.
> For the darkness shall turn to dawning, and the dawning to noon-day bright,
> And Christ's great kingdom shall come on earth, the kingdom of love and light.
> We've a song to be sung to the nations that shall lift their hearts to the Lord,
> A song that shall conquer evil and shatter the spear and sword.
> We've a message to give to the nations, that the Lord who reigneth above,
> Hath sent us His Son to save us, and show us that God is love.
> We've a Savior to show to the nations, who the path of sorrow hath trod,
> That all of the world's great peoples, might come to the truth of God.

This is the cry of my heart as I share my walk with the Lord with you. Be encouraged. God is real and He waits to be gracious to His people (Isa. 30:18–19).

PART I:
Preparing the Bride of Christ

CHAPTER 1

To Be Prepared

"Are you ready?"

I heard a voice speak these powerful words while I was in a deep sleep. Startled by the words, I woke up. Who was speaking? My first thought suggested the man with whom my husband and I were staying in South Africa. I waited for a response, but saw no-one was there. Then I knew I'd heard the audible voice of the Lord.

This stirred my spirit deeply, as the Lord has been speaking to me about the end-time harvest. He's asking us at this time: "Are you ready?"

People of God; we live in a strategic hour of history. The Lord is calling us to prepare for this time. We must align ourselves with God to receive His blessing and not His judgment. Our assignment will flow out of our intimate walk with God.

The Lord has many different assignments for His children. Each of us has different gifts, and the Lord gives us different callings. We read in Hosea 4:6: "My people are destroyed from lack of knowledge." We need to search the heart of God. God asks a critical question in the book of Joel: "The Day of the Lord is great; it is dreadful, who can endure it?" (Joel 2:11b).

We are on a journey of understanding God's heart and His plan for the end of the age. "Are you ready?"

Your Light Has Come

Shortly after I heard the Lord's voice, my senior pastor gave me a large, prophetic painting that took my breath away. He felt the Lord wanted me to have the painting as a personal and corporate word. The picture illustrates the words "Arise, shine", from Isaiah 60:1.

A warrior woman sits on a cliff clad in armor, and a lion sits beside her. The woman's eyes are filled with confidence and strength. The sky is dark and wild. The following quote came with the picture:

> "Although darkness is coming over the earth,
> The Lion and the woman in this painting
> Survey the scene with calm victory,
> Alert, but at rest.
> They are lit by the sun
> Though storms surround them.
> 'Your light has come-
> The glory of the Lord rises upon you.
> Lift up your eyes and look about you.'
> Understand the times and the glory you are called to."

I felt the Spirit of God covering this message and hung the painting under the spotlight in my foyer. For weeks, every time I walked by the painting, I read the message and the power of God fell on me. I would weep, feeling a deep yearning in my spirit. What does it mean to be ready for the darkness that is coming over the earth? Will we have calm victory, alert, but at rest? Do we understand the times that are coming and the glory we're called to? The Lord wants to ready His bride.

A Bride Not Ready

I've received several dreams from the Lord about my wedding day. In one dream, I was supposed to walk down the aisle in two hours, and I didn't have a wedding dress. In another dream the bridesmaids didn't have their dresses, and the wedding was later that day. In a third dream, it was the evening rehearsal before the wedding. The reception, hall, and food weren't arranged. Although I was the bride, I wasn't ready for my wedding day. I awoke in a panic. I took these dreams to mean that the Lord is calling His bride to make herself ready for His return.

Different seasons in our lives come as we mature, and now the Lord is calling his bride into the season of preparation. When the Lord's power enters into time, we are empowered by His grace and situations change. Life becomes different.

The Body of Christ doesn't have an understanding of the full concept of judgment. When God ends one season and begins another, or takes us through transition, He has to bring some old situations to an end. This is why the tribe of Issachar understood their time. The people knew how certain structures had to end so that the new season God had planned would begin.

God wants us to understand and interpret the different seasons of our lives so we can prosper and gain wisdom to advance to the next one.

As we understand the season in which we live as the sons of Issachar did (1 Chron. 12:32), we can advance into this new season when the Lord is calling His bride to make herself ready. However, let us rest and operate from God's peace.

Hidden in Him

> He who dwells in the shelter of the Most High
> will rest in the shadow of the Almighty.
> I will say of the Lord, "He is my refuge and my fortress,
> My God, in whom I trust."
>
> Surely he will save you from the fowler's snare
> And from the deadly pestilence.
> He will cover you with his feathers,
> And under his wings you will find refuge:
> His faithfulness will be your shield and rampart.
> You will not fear the terror of night,
> Nor the arrow that flies by day,

Nor the pestilence that stalks in the darkness,
Nor the plague that destroys at midday.
A thousand may fall at your side,
Ten thousand at your right hand,
But it will not come near you.
You will only observe with your eyes
And see the punishment of the wicked. (Ps. 91:1–8)

As God's children, we must remain hidden under His wings, and in that "hiddenness" we are divinely protected from our enemies. Then we can be confident we're safe. His angels guard us while we make the Most High our dwelling. He desires to speak to each of us in the secret place and unveils many mysteries. There He reveals hidden revelations needed for such a time as this.

If you make the Most High your dwelling—
Even the Lord, who is my refuge—
Then no harm will befall you,
No disaster will come near your tent.
For he will command his angels concerning you
To guard you in all your ways;
They will lift you up in their hands,
So that you will not strike your foot against a stone.
You will tread upon the lion and the cobra:
You will trample the great lion and the serpent.

"Because he loves me," says the Lord,
"I will rescue him; I will protect him, for he acknowledges my name.
He will call upon me, and I will answer him;
I will be with him in trouble,
I will deliver him and honor him.
With long life will I satisfy him and show him my salvation."
(Ps. 91:9-16)

We're called to rest in the shadow of the Almighty. Though storms surround us, the glory of the Lord rises on us. We must lift our eyes, look around us, and understand the times in which we live. We're called to witness to the glory of God and to "arise and shine." The Lord wants our suffering to reveal His glory in us (Rom. 8:18). The Lord desires His glory to be released across our land.

His purpose is to raise up the name of Jesus, and for all people to know His glory, majesty, greatness, faithfulness, immeasurable love, long suffering and patience. As we get to know each of His attributes through the Holy Spirit within us, we comprehend who He is.

Proven Character Through Adversity

God wants us to know Him through our suffering, using even the most painful situations for His glory and our good. "But the people who know their God shall be strong, and carry out great exploits" (Dan. 11:32 NKJV). God wants us to do great things for His kingdom. As we get to know Him through understanding how to deal with suffering, we can achieve great exploits for His glory. Then others will see the work of our great God and desire to serve Him.

When we're young in Christ, God accepts us as babes. However, there comes a time, when He begins to deal with us as sons and daughters. As in the physical, so it is in the spiritual there is a process of maturing. The ultimate call is to be the mature, spotless bride.

During this time of preparation we're led into battle, and the war is over the purity of our heart. Before Jesus was led to do wonders, He was led to do battle. The Father proved the character of His Son through conflict. He was tempted. Tempted actually means "tested" or "proven in adversity." As we grasp this concept, we are able to endure and overcome through God's empowering grace.

Unity and Prayer

Prayer becomes our heart beat the more we mature in His love. Then we know our call to prayer. We're called to pray to usher in the kingdom of heaven to this earth. The Lord has set this forth in His model prayer in Matthew 6:10: "Your kingdom come, your will be done, on earth as it is in heaven." Prayer is an important part of God's move in this hour. The Lord is placing His burden on many hearts to usher in His presence.

By praying together in unity of spirit we carry much authority. Being with one another in presence is conformity, but not necessarily unity. We must come together in one accord—in heart and mind in the Holy Spirit—as we see lived out in Acts 4:32.

Deuteronomy 32:30 teaches us that one can chase a thousand but two can put ten thousand to flight. We also know that where there is unity God commands a blessing (Ps. 133:1–30). In Acts 4:24 we see a prayer of agreement: "When they heard this, they raised their voices together in prayer to God."

Through a divine connection my husband and I met a man from Capetown, South Africa with a divine call to bring unity in prayer to all the nations in the world. In 2007, we were honored to have him speak in our city. Graham Powers began the Global Day of Prayer in response to the Lord's calling. The morning he spoke, the Lord spoke to me from His Word: "My Glory will cover this land." God's power hit me like an electric shock.

During Graham's testimony later that morning, he shared how the Lord first called him to start the Global Day of Prayer. He described the experience by saying: "it was like electricity hit me." This touched me as I had just experienced that electric shock before he spoke.

The Lord called Graham to this ministry and in 2009 all nations were in prayer on the same day for the first time in history. This is the call to prayer as God's people come together and call upon His name with one heart and one mind.

Intercession

I understood from the Lord the importance of prayer through reading many books on intercession. My spirit acquired a new urgency on reading Kenneth E. Hagin's book, *The Art of Intercession*. The first chapter in his book is "Why Pray?"

> Years ago I read a statement John Wesley made and it stayed with me. Wesley said, "It seems God is limited by our prayer life—that He can do nothing for humanity unless someone asks Him."
>
> A while later, in 1949, I was reading after another writer who made that same statement. But this fellow added, "Why this is, I do not know."
>
> "Why doesn't he know?" I asked. Then I found out I didn't know either.
>
> Yet if Wesley's statement is correct—and it seems to be as you read through the Bible—then we who are to pray should know more about it.
>
> I began to examine the Bible to find out why, if God wants to do something for humanity, He cannot unless somebody asks Him. I found the answer through study of God's Word.
>
> You see, though some people have built up "spiritual air castles" that God is running everything in this world, He is not.

He concludes the chapter:

> I saw that God made the world and the fullness thereof. He made His man, Adam.
>
> Then He said, "Adam, I give you dominion over all the work of my hands" (Gen. 1:26 and 27; Ps. 8:6).
>
> God did not say, "I am going to dominate through you."

He said, "I give you dominion over all the work of my hands." Therefore Adam had dominion upon this earth and in this world. He was originally, in a sense, god of this world.

But Satan came and lied to Adam. Adam committed high treason and sold out to Satan and he became the god of this world.

2 Corinthians 4:4 calls Satan "the god of this world." As such, he has dominion. Where? In this world.

He will have that dominion; he will be god of this world, until Adam's lease runs out.

God cannot legally and justly move in and take away that dominion from the devil. The devil has dominion here. He has a right. He has Adam's lease. And God cannot do anything unless somebody down here asks Him.

These great men of God, who have gone before us, understood and knew the power and importance of prayer. I was so blessed reading their testimonies, it gave me the sense of responsibility we have as God's children, especially now. I feel the urgent call to prayer, because prayer moves the hand of God when we are aligned with Him.

The Glory of His Kingdom

What is the urgent need? To pray for the Holy Spirit to come and fill our hearts, the hearts of our families, churches, cities, and our nations: that His Glory will cover our land. The forces of the enemy are gaining strength, but "greater is He that is in us than he that is in the world" (1 John 4:4). The war against the hordes of darkness is not won by using our own resources, but by releasing the light. Then darkness has to flee. As we release the light, God's glory will cover our land.

What is God's glory? God's glory is the outward radiance of the intrinsic beauty of His holiness, and the greatness of his manifold perfections. What is our hope? Seeing the Glory of God. Recall the following Scriptures:

"We boast in the hope of the glory of God." (Romans 5:2)

God will "present you before His glorious presence without fault and with great joy." (Jude 24)

He will "make the riches of His glory known to the objects of his mercy, whom He prepared in advance for glory." (Rom. 9:23)

"Who calls you into His kingdom and glory." (1 Thess. 2:12)

"While we wait for the blessed hope—the glorious appearing of our great God and Savior, Jesus Christ." (Titus 2:13)

God wants us to manifest His glory.

God calls us into His kingdom and glory. He not only wants us in His kingdom but also to be filled with the glory of His kingdom. Then it can be released and cover our land from sea to sea, and fulfill the promises of His Word.

As we seek higher levels of God's glory, it is essential to remain properly placed in His divine presence. Being properly placed means staying "hidden" in Christ. He covers us with His wings and hides us in Himself. In the secret place God reveals His secret plans and gives us strategies to overcome the enemy, and achieve victory. It is here we develop a passion to understand the mysteries of God. From this resting place we move from faith to faith, strength to strength, and glory to glory.

But whenever anyone turns to the Lord, the veil is taken away. Now the Lord is the Spirit, and where the Spirit of the Lord is, there is freedom. And we, who with unveiled faces all reflect the Lord's glory, are being transformed into his

likeness with ever increasing glory, which comes from the
Lord, who is the Spirit. (2 Cor. 3: 16–18)

As we gain new levels of faith, God gives us strength for each new
level and empowers us to embrace greater levels of His glory. As my
faith grew, He empowered me to be an overcomer in the battle, and so
I began to embrace the glory. As I came to experience greater levels, His
glory hit me. I collapsed, groaning in His presence.

When we embrace the presence of God, prayer becomes our very
heart beat. Humbling ourselves before Him pleases God; in this attitude
He can use us to heal our land.

> If my people, who are called by my name, will humble
> themselves and pray and seek my face, and turn from their
> wicked ways, then will I hear from heaven and will forgive
> their sin and will heal their land. (2 Chr. 7:14)

As we repent in humility before our Father in Heaven and turn
from our wicked ways, He promises to hear us and forgive our sins and
heal our land. We will bear His glory as our hearts gain an increasing
measure of purity before the Lord. He is coming back for His spotless
Bride, but His Bride must make herself ready (Rev. 19:7b).

Our Comfort Zone Expands as We Mature

Becoming ready is a process of maturing. As we mature from child
to adult, we endure trials and respond by trusting our loving Father
who knows our every need. So we mature spiritually. As we overcome,
the Lord brings us out of our comfort zone into new levels of service.
This was my experience, and has been the experience of many others.

After a Sunday morning service, as I talked to a friend by the front
door of the church, a woman came up to me and introduced herself.

"Are you Mrs. Van Hierden?"

"Yes, I am." I replied.

She went on, "Are you Amanda and Carlarene's mother?"

I was puzzled and curious, wondering what she was leading to.

"Yes, I am," I answered.

"We want you to speak at our next women's conference," she said.

This bold statement, rather than a question, startled and bewildered me and took my breath away, leaving me briefly speechless.

Finally I said, "I'm not a public speaker."

Standing in front of a crowd frightened me. The thought of speaking made me weak at the knees and feeling my throat would close. But what should I do with this statement? It was not a question.

I said it one more time. "I'm not a public speaker."

If I said it a second time she might get the hint; it's not who I am and possibly back off. But she was determined.

She said, "Oh, that's okay, I have a book for you to read on public speaking."

Next time I saw her, she handed me the book by Peter Daniels about his journey into public speaking. His testimony was stirring and my heart began to awaken for what the Lord had for me. This woman would not hear the word "no" because I sensed she was speaking under the Spirit's anointing. God was gripping my heart; it was out of my comfort zone and scared me. I knew I must join a toastmaster group, (a public speaking club) as soon as possible.

I've always been more involved with "hands on" gifting: playing organ in Sunday school at age twelve; playing in church at thirteen. I started drawing in the first grade and became a painting artist, going on to displaying and selling art in museums, galleries, and at art in the park. I won trophies in sewing at age eleven, sewing most of what my three sisters and my mother and I wore. I made and decorated wedding cakes for almost every wedding I attended. That was fulfilling enough for me; that's where I found my pleasure. I considered my gifting as using my hands, not in speaking or writing. This was a box I had put myself in. Was God calling me out of the box?

My husband had asked me many times to be part of the Christian toastmaster club that he and another man had founded. Without knowing the call of the Lord on my life, I had no desire to join any club, and thought there was no reason to be involved with anything vocal. But I joined another toastmaster club and spoke seven times in six months. It was enough for me to gain confidence to address a crowd and be part of contests within the club.

The Lord wants our lives to be completely surrendered to Him, even if it stretches us more than we think possible. It's all about honoring and glorifying our Savior and our Lord. He is the Lord of our lives. As we surrender our lives, He may ask us to move from our old paradigms and embrace God's new thing, moving from glory to glory. We must welcome a new level of faith rather than go against His new direction. I need constantly to remind myself of God's new direction for my life and confidently walk by His grace! Sometimes radical behavior is required during these changing seasons. Pursuing His glory gives us grace to be obedient to any new thing God has for us.

> Forget the former things; do not dwell on the past. See, I am doing a new thing! Now it springs up; do you not perceive it? I am making a way in the desert and streams in the wasteland. (Is. 43:18–19)

CHAPTER 2

Not Ready for the Harvest

In November 2007 my husband Peter and I spent two weeks in Huntley, Scotland. We attended a school entitled, "Healing of the Land," about transformation for the nations. At lunch on the first day, Alistair Petrie, the teacher, announced:

"We will not have our next session at 2:00, God wants to speak to His people. We will have the next session at 4:00."

I immediately tuned into this message. What was God going to release to His people? My anticipation began to grow. I had a sober excitement waiting on God. Our teacher was tuning into God and now I must also tune in to hear His voice. God is speaking! Would He speak to me?

My hunger for His presence grew as I looked for a place to be alone. I wanted no distractions. Where could I be alone in such a busy place? Checking each room as I walked the hall, I entered a room that seemed quiet. I finally settled behind a little table in the back of a beautiful Scottish style tea room. I needed to be apart from the noise of students sharing the excitement of our gathering.

I sat down and asked the Lord, "What do you want me to do? Do you want me to pray, read your Word, journal, read a book from my book bag?" Before any more thought, as jet lag was hitting me, I laid my Bible down on the floor. The soft cover gave the impression of a soft pillow, and soon I was sound asleep with my head resting on the cover.

I began to dream.

I walked into a large room filled with little children, and quickly realized it was a day care center. The children were peacefully playing. A cupboard in the back of the room had a small utility sink with a high spout, and I walked over to wash my hair. I found some shampoo and worked it into a lather on my head, the urge to wash was satisfied and I was feeling refreshed. With no towel to wrap my head, I left the room with my hair dripping.

Outside I saw a door to another building and opened it. Inside, the busy activity of women everywhere overwhelmed me. They placed frying pans over a fire that extended down the center of the room in a large brick fire pit with an overhanging hood. The women were all sizes and heights, and each one wore a bibbed apron. There was no room for me, and it felt dangerous for me to enter any further. I grabbed a towel I spotted and wrapped it on my head to stop water from my wet hair dripping into my eyes.

Outside again, I saw a trailer with an abnormally large hay bale attached to a tractor. The trailer rode low and looked easy to hop on. Feeling bewildered and a little lost, I thought the trailer might give me a sense of direction, especially when my brother walked toward the tractor. As he prepared to drive off, I jumped on with the hay bale and was soon bouncing down the lane. To the left of the road I observed a variety of farm equipment including combines, swathers, and bailers. I wondered how they avoided colliding, because it was so busy. A sense of guilt hit me as I remembered my present state. What was I doing? As I awoke, the Lord clearly spoke to me "YOU ARE NOT READY FOR THE HARVEST!" I came to, sharply startled.

I couldn't make sense of my dream, but it left a deep impression on me and I could hardly speak as I went to find my husband. What was the Lord telling me? "I wasn't ready for the harvest"? In the dream the harvest was going on. I wandered with no purpose, not knowing where to go, with no sense of direction. I felt like a lost puppy. Things were happening and I was not part of it. The only words spoken during the whole dream were, "You are not ready for the harvest." During the next few days of the school I wondered, pondered, prayed, and entreated the Lord. What could all this mean?

At the end of that week we went to another city. The first night there I had three dreams of instruction. I share with you the one that relates to the dream regarding the harvest.

I was sitting together with another woman at a conference. Suddenly, she reached over and picked up my right hand. She pointed out that the little finger on my right hand was a stub. I began to feel it with my left hand. As I moved to my fourth finger, it was also a stub. Then the middle finger was a stub, broken off below the knuckle. I felt devastated as I touched the next finger and then my thumb. Then I began feeling each finger on my left hand one by one and each one was also a stub. I rubbed and rolled my hands together in fright, and awoke to find I was still rubbing my hands and checking my fingers. As I woke I heard the words, "You are mal-nutritious."

God spoke to me in this dream, but I couldn't understand its meaning for several years. Later, I received revelation. In light of the end time Bride, I saw I was not ready for the harvest. The Lord was also telling me I am mal-nutritious. Being mal-nourished is to not receive nourishment from what I consume. Further, being mal-nutritious, I failed to give to others the nourishment I had received. As children of God we must continually strengthen others in their walk with God.

I felt the weight of my insufficiency, my lack of understanding, my confusion. I didn't know what to do with this revelation or who could help me understand it. I wanted to know what God was saying to me; I felt like such a little child. *O Daddy! I just cannot understand all these things.*

Now I see this is a message in line with the charge of God on my life to release the message of God's grace and glory. I must give the word of my testimony in light of the message that came with such power, "We've a story to tell to the Nations." It is only by His grace that we release His glory. I pray my testimony may be an encouragement to God's people and also bring many to the Lord that do not know Him. Seek Him while He may be found.

Continued Revelation

We returned from our trip and a couple of days later I had a third dream. I was working in a store and my husband, Peter, came to visit me. When he entered the back room I did not recognize him. I was shocked. He looked like a dead man walking. He stopped long enough to tell me good-bye as he was off on a trip to China.

At this I awoke. I felt I had no interpretation for this dream. The weight of this message hung heavy on my heart; I felt ready to burst. The Lord gave me a husband with much spiritual gifting and a deep desire to walk intimately with Him. As I explained this dream to him, he immediately gave me the interpretation. He said, "If you don't walk in your call, I will not be able to walk in my call."

As revelation came to me, I understood the Lord was instructing me with the call to prayer and that Peter couldn't walk into his destiny without the cover of prayer. We must walk together in unity, praying for cover, instruction, and direction.

Then I felt I couldn't handle any more instruction without the Lord giving me direction about the meaning of this message. My hunger was so intense my whole body and mind was screaming inside. I was compelled to say, "Lord, here I am." I felt like a weak broken vessel in the hands of the potter, a lump of clay. I just wanted to hear from the Lord. The yearning was so deep, I could do nothing but wait before the Lord. My life came to a standstill with only that one focus. It was urgent!

Praying for Interpretation of the Revelation

That morning, I prayed with a woman who I prayed with every week by phone. We talked and I explained all this to her and she said that as long as I was speaking she kept getting, "two weeks, two weeks, two weeks." I felt this only added to all the questions that were weighing me down. What was I to do with this kind of an answer? It made no sense. Then she said, "Janet, the Lord is going to reveal everything to you in the next two weeks." I replaced the phone.

I said to Peter, "Honey, I am going to take the van and find a quiet spot somewhere. I must hear what God is saying. I can't go on; I'm ready to explode."

I took my van and went to a quiet place. I parked and set the seats down in the middle, went into the back seat, and as I put my hand into my book bag I said, "Lord I need to hear from you!" As I prayed that short prayer, the power of God came down on me like a huge dump of water. I could hardly breathe. It was the power of God, the Holy Spirit. I was sitting in the presence of the maker of heaven and earth. I was in awe before the Lord, not able to speak or move. I knew the Lord had a powerful word for me. There are times He whispers and times He speaks loudly and with much power. This was one of those moments that seemed He shook the whole earth.

Gasping for breath, I pulled the book out from my book bag. It was a book by Kenneth Hagin, *The Church Triumphant*. The bookmark in the middle of the book was at the chapter entitled "Vision of the Frogs." Kenneth wrote how the Lord often invites us to pray for mercy from the Lord's judgment upon another person. If we are not obedient to the call to prayer, Kenneth wrote, we are held responsible and the judgment will come upon us. He gave an example. If the President of the United States does things not pleasing to the Lord, the Lord may call us to pray for him. If we do not pray when God asks, then that judgment will be upon us before His judgment seat. I hadn't heard anything like this before, and would have thought it to be heresy if I was not overwhelmed with the presence of God. With that intensity of the Holy Spirit I knew the Lord was speaking and I must pay attention. I felt I was drowning, yet felt an incredible peace with the message. The ambiguity was heavy in my mind and spirit, and I was puzzled. But I realized there was more to come, and thought I could go home and wait upon the Lord to hear more from Him.

On returning home, I asked Peter to pray and ask the Lord if there was more.

He answered, "Yes, I sense there is more."

I immediately felt the book *Praying with Fire* by Barbara Billet was part of what the Lord was telling me. The Lord was calling me to prayer. The burden was there, but I did not understand how it would come about. I was overwhelmed with the concept of prayer, as it was new, uncharted territory for me.

Fight Well

With Peter's interpretation of my third dream: "If you don't walk in your call, I will not be able to walk in my call," I began to receive revelation regarding my husband. The instruction was to pray together in unity, for God's destiny, cover, instruction, and direction. This was to fight the good fight, holding on to the faith and a good conscience together. As one puts a thousand to flight and two put ten thousand to flight, for us to walk in our destiny, revealed by the prophetic word spoken over us, we must not just fight, but fight the *good* fight.

> "Timothy, my son, I give you this instruction in keeping with the prophecies once made about you, so that by following them you may fight the good fight, holding on to faith and a good conscience. Some have rejected these and so have shipwrecked their faith." (1 Tim. 1:18–19)

Other versions use the word warfare. The KJV says, "War a good warfare." The ESV reads, "Wage the good warfare." The NLT provides more understanding of the Lord's word to us: "Fight well in the Lord's battles." Prayer is where this battle, this warfare, and this fight will be won. We cannot walk in our destiny and this battle without wearing the armor of God.

> Finally, be strong in the Lord and in his mighty power. Put on the full armor of God so that you can take your stand against the devil's schemes. For our struggle is not against flesh and blood, but against the rulers, against the authorities, against the powers of this dark world and against the spiritual forces of evil in the heavenly realms. Therefore put on the full armor of God, so that when the day of evil

comes, you may be able to stand your ground . . . (Eph. 6:10–17)

We cannot expect a prophetic word to happen without this battle. A prophetic word is the will of the Lord for us and must be birthed in prayer. Many prophetic words fall to the ground because we do not know how to respond. We need to be diligent, bring revelation to birth, and win the battle; to walk out the revelation in consistent obedience or the prophecies will flounder.

Not understanding what the prophetic word was about and what to do with it, I needed to understand it from the Word of God. I saw we cannot just receive it, and sit back and wait for its fulfillment, but it is a word that needs to be birthed in battle or it will not come to pass.

With much grief, I've seen many of God's people, with very high prophetic words spoken to them, never walk in their destiny. It is only by the amazing grace of God that any of us are able to be an overcomer and fulfill the call of the Lord on our lives. We often become offended at God when we've sat back and waited for the "word" to happen and found it did not. Whether they are words from someone or words the Lord gives to us, any revelation needs to be birthed.

To Be Purified

Before the promises of the Lord come to pass, there will often be unexpected preparation on our part to purify us, before the Lord can use us. This refining needs to happen to mature us enough to walk in our destiny, and may take many months or years. We must be willing to be refined by the Lord, and ready to pay the price. It may cost us friendships, positions at work, family or church relationships, material possessions, personal dreams, or plans for the future. But as the Lord prepares us for the end time harvest He will refine us, mold us, and conform us further into His image, to be available for His glory. He will make us "ready" to be the bride of Christ, purified for His coming.

As we are sanctified we are purified, so we can take the kingdom. He who takes the kingdom takes the harvest. The harvest is whoever responds to the kingdom.

Our mandate in this season is to receive the clarion call to be made ready to prepare the way. Let's receive the prophetic challenge and pick up the baton; to be those who are not only prepared, but who also prepare a way for others to receive God's glory.

Compassion

If we are to fully understand prayer, we need an understanding of compassion. First, we need the compassion of Jesus and then pray compassion prayers that flow from the heart of Jesus.

The Lord revealed this to me through a series of events, beginning with a visit to a church we attended while away from home. As I walked in I noticed a small table with a few books laid out for sale. I randomly touched one of the books with my finger tips. As I did, I felt the power of God come down on my head, go down my arm and out my finger tips onto this book.

My body shook and I said to my husband, "I think I am supposed to read this book."

He asked, "What is it?" He looked at it. "Yes," he agreed, "You're to read this book."

I was eager to know what this book was about. The book was by James W. and Michal Ann Goll, entitled *Compassion*.

I read most of the book during the drive home, and while stretching my legs at a gas station, it occurred to me that the next day was two weeks since my friend had predicted the Lord would give me revelation in two weeks regarding her prophetic word from the Lord. I was to wait upon the Lord and hear from Him. I burst out with such joy and adoration of who God is. I stood there for a moment as I marvelled how God had fulfilled His promise. My heart was overwhelmed with praise. The truths of this book penetrated my spirit. Understanding the compassion of Jesus was beginning to captivate me. David Ruis writes, "As followers of Jesus, we cannot ignore what moved Him to send out the first of His disciples, what moves Him still to send us out today: compassion. Biblical compassion is a uniquely Christian virtue."

Jesus always saw the need first, then He was moved with a compassion so strong that it always led Him to do something in response. Matthew writes, "When He saw the throngs, He was moved with pity and sympathy for them, because they were bewildered—harassed and distressed and dejected and helpless—like sheep without a shepherd" (Matt. 9:36, Amplified Version).

The Greek word for compassion (pity and sympathy) that is used here is 'splanchnizomai', and it means "to be moved deep within." It involves a sense of yearning on behalf of others. We will take action, as Jesus was, if we're filled with compassion. God is our loving heavenly Father, and He wants us to be filled with that same powerful compassion. As David Ruis writes:

> "To touch Christ is to touch compassion. Far beyond a guilt-trip, a tweaked conscience or a pale sense of pity, compassion reaches into the very guts and demands action. It compels prayers that will move heaven, intercessions that cry out for workers to be thrust into this weighted-down harvest. It motivates one to move—to go and set it right—to administer justice through the power of the Kingdom."

Compassion is a deep well that moves Heaven on behalf of others.

Christ's Compassion Felt

God places great value on our tears. One day I was weeping with my elbows on the window sill upstairs, gazing across the countryside, and wondering if the Lord heard me. I did not feel His presence; I felt deserted and lonely. The next day a couple that had our names from a mutual friend came to visit us. They were told to stop in and stay with us. She was in our home for only a few minutes before she said,

"Janet, the Lord saw you with your elbows on the window sill. He saw you weeping, and He took every tear and put it in a bottle!" She was reminding me of Psalm 56:8: "You have collected all my tears in your bottle. You have recorded each one in your book." (NLT).

I was so moved by those prophetic words, I never again thought the Lord did not see me. Even when I do not sense His presence I know He is there and that He is moved with compassion when I hurt. I no longer doubted the Lord was watching over me every moment. The Lord sent a messenger to tell me, to relieve my doubts for good.

I began to learn that as we go forth in compassion, we cannot go simply with sympathy and pity. We need to teach others how to overcome through faith, prayer, and spiritual understanding. We need to exemplify Kingdom authority right out in the open as Jesus did for all to see. The kind of compassion Jesus demonstrated was not weak and passive; it was tender yet tough, sensitive yet confrontational.

Sometimes we need to be soft and gentle and bring healing. Other times we must be drastic and bold, cutting between soul and spirit with the living Word. As we walk in faith, knowing God's attributes, His nature, who we are in Christ, and how much God is enthralled with us, we enter into prayer that eventually becomes our very heart beat. We talk to God as our dearest friend, knowing that we are not complete without Him at our side.

So we grow in our spiritual understanding because of our communion with God, as we get to know God in each Person—Father, Son and Holy Spirit. The following chapter will explain the journey the Lord took me on to know each Person of the Godhead.

Through the knowledge of God we can walk in Kingdom authority and do what God has placed us on earth to do. It is only through intimacy with Him that we will walk out the assignment He has for each of us. This work is difficult if we try it in the flesh; it is only with the Holy Spirit and we receive a constant flow of God's grace, that this will work out.

As the Lord teaches us these concepts we must reach out, teach others, and come along side in the spirit of "compassion" as they open themselves up to receive. If we truly love someone we will be faithful with them, as iron will sharpen iron. We help each other mature. We need others to be faithful to us. We are wise when we receive rebuke. "Do not rebuke a mocker or he will hate you; rebuke a wise man and he will love you" (Prov. 9:8). "Let a righteous man strike me—it is a kindness; let him rebuke me—it is oil on my head. My head will not refuse it" (Ps. 141:5).

If we do not receive rebuke, and we become angry or offended, the Word says we are not wise. Are we teachable and open to grow in the wisdom of the Lord? A person that will not receive rebuke places himself in jeopardy. When we are controlled by the Spirit, we respond to the Holy Spirit speaking to us and we follow Him in obedience. We are to use gentleness to come around the person that is overtaken in misconduct. We see this concept in Galatians.

> "Brethren, if any person is overtaken in misconduct or sin of any sort, you who are spiritual (who are responsive to and controlled by the Spirit) should set him right and restore and reinstate him, without any sense of superiority and with all gentleness . . . (Gal. 6:1 Amplified Version)

Battle Against the Enemy

We find that "to the one we are the smell of death; to the other, the fragrance of life" (2 Cor. 2: 16a). When we speak forth the Words of Life, we may be rejected. Some choose to receive and others choose not to. Only the Holy Spirit can work repentance. We can only deliver the words of life and pray they will fall on soft soil that will receive them.

I faced a very strange situation with a young woman while attending a Bible study and prayer meeting. She made an accusation against me that shocked me and everyone in the room. This situation could have caused an upheaval and much division. It was so disrespectful, I did not know how to start gentle restoration.

When I arrived home I came to the Lord.

"What was that all about?" I asked.

His immediate response: "I want you to laugh at the devil." . . . but the Lord laughs at the wicked, for he knows their day is coming (Ps. 37:13).

What? Laugh? I was stunned at that response. I hadn't understood that before, and didn't take it lightly, but I knew the Lord was allowing the enemy to put me through a test to mature me in spiritual warfare. I needed to love her with the compassion of Jesus in the face of her accusation for others to recognize her error and see I was unfazed. I did not need to defend myself with one word. I know who I am in Christ and my conscience was clear of the offence. These events must cause us to walk with him so all accusations are shed like water off a duck's back. "For it is God's will that by doing good you should silence the ignorant talk of foolish men" (1 Peter 2:15).

My conduct would prove it was a false accusation. I needed to display the "love walk," the walk of compassion that is not natural to humans, but displayed from within by God's Spirit. Then the Lord revealed to me it was a testimony to people when an accusation is false and we can walk in peace and feel unharmed. If we confront someone with a given sin and they do not receive it, they will often accuse us of judging them. It soothes their conscience to shift the blame.

The Lord's assignment was for me to understand how to withstand the enemy and restore the person: to see the enemy, and separately, to see the person, and restore the person to walk in freedom through the heart of compassion. This was a test for me to walk through Galatians 6:1 in obedience and by His grace. "Brothers, if someone is caught in a sin, you who are spiritual should restore him gently . . ." I needed to overcome and restore this woman by walking intimately with the Lord. I saw complete restoration. Trust was built through this attempt of the enemy to destroy our relationship. The enemy lost this battle, and today we have a strong friendship.

We need to walk through this, to speak it to others with authority. May this testimony bring glory to the Holy Spirit and His work within us. Let compassion flow out of our innermost being. By practicing His presence compassion is born. The love of God works within us, and as it works inward, it always begins to move outward.

People of Compassion

I was blessed by the many testimonies written by James W. and Michal Ann Goll in their book *Compassion,* including those that follow of Catherine Booth, Mother Teresa, and Heidi Baker.

The Mother of the Salvation Army, Catherine Booth, was a true heroine of faith and compassion. I was blessed to see how her life blended together with her husband. William and Catherine exemplified a Barak and Deborah type anointing (Judges 4 and 5). The ministry and anointing of each made the other possible. I believe this anointing is being released today—serving together, working together, benefiting each other, jealous only for the illumination and the presence of our God. The Lord spoke the same message to me in the dream of instruction; my husband would not be able to walk in his call if I did not walk in mine, so our call together was clear. The Lord frequently calls a husband and wife, or even a family, together as a team.

Catherine Booth knew that compassion is an action, not just a feeling, and it is born out of passion for the Father's heart. She wrote, "Don't let controversy hurt your soul. Live near to God by prayer. Just fall down at his feet and open your very soul before him, and throw yourself right into his arms." The testimony I shared, of walking through with this young woman, was first compassion with a feeling and then compassion walked out as the Lord gave me grace; compassion in action. Walking in the understanding of the Father's heart with this young woman, included forgiveness and compassion, and peace within myself. I knew who I am in Christ and His work perfected in me. Only the work of the Holy Spirit within gives strength to endure every battle we face. He is to be glorified.

Mother Teresa was probably the most compassionate person of the twentieth century. She reached out with compassion from Calcutta, India, among the poor, to the rich and famous all around the world.

She exhibited the qualities of humility, love, and compassion wherever she went. She was known as the "angel of mercy" to the poor. An angel is a messenger, one who is always ready to come to the aid of others.

She found her strength in prayer and in the silent contemplation of Jesus Christ. Her ministry to the orphans was pure and unblemished, and she kept herself uncontaminated by the world. She developed her parenting skills by getting to know her heavenly Father. Everyone who knew her saw she had a personal and intimate relationship with her heavenly Father. Mother Teresa taught forgiveness as an important part of compassion; she became something beautiful for God.

This humble woman who came from a poor, obscure village in Macedonia, rose to become a most respected woman because she was faithful to God's call. She devoted her life to serving others. She was a role model of compassion for all to follow. Only as we are able to empathize with and understand the person who has wronged us, will we be able to forgive them and find peace for ourselves.

Heidi Baker is a modern-day evangelist of compassion who is living this call. She lives with her husband Roland in Mozambique. Heidi radiates the love, compassion, and the joy of the Lord to everyone with whom she comes in contact. She calls herself a "laid down lover of God," one whose life is wholly given over to the Lord, whose life inspires others to surrender more completely to the love and service of Jesus. Heidi released these words at a Voice of the Apostles conference in 2005, "Fully possessed by the Holy Spirit we become lovers and we do radical things because we know who we are." Heidi has no formula for raising the dead except that she literally loves people back to life. She has held the dead bodies of babies and others, weeping over them for hours, until warmth came back into them and they were supernaturally revived. This is true compassion in action.

Heidi knows how much she is loved by the Father and through that she is able to do extreme acts of compassion. This knowledge is one of the keys to walk in the level of compassion God calls us to. As we walk in intimacy with Him and know who we are in Christ, we welcome the Holy Spirit into our lives. As I began to walk in the understanding of who I am in Christ, it changed my life. My focus became Christ centered instead of self-centered. What people said about me did not have the same impact; I'm focused on what God thinks of me.

Compassion Prayer

These testimonies demonstrate, as believers, we must find a personal way to plant seeds of compassion wherever we go. The Holy Spirit is looking for champions today. Whether we are great or small the Lord wants us to know Him and to do great exploits. Compassion is always personal, it costs something but it releases something. I came to understand compassion is not only a feeling, but also an action that radiates from us as Christ is formed in us. So Holy Spirit compassion came upon me.

My son and I were driving on the freeway near our home when a noisy car passing us caught our attention. Stressed by his day at school, my son made a negative comment about the car. The compassion of Jesus hit me and I began to weep in intercession. I felt I needed to cry out to the Lord, to pray for the young driver, for his salvation and finances. I asked the Lord to bless him financially, to have mercy on him and draw him towards Himself. The feeling of compassion overwhelmed me and immediately caused me to well up in powerful prayer, weeping. Then I pulled up beside the car.

"Mom, what are you doing?" my son asked.

"I need to see what he looks like because I am going to see him in Heaven." I said.

The burden of prayer was so deep, I knew God had a purpose for this unusual occasion. This individual needed prayer. My son was touched by the Lord's compassion and sat speechless as we continued to drive. He was drinking in the presence of God and it made a lasting impact on him. When we arrived he was in deep thought; the Spirit of God was so heavy that he didn't get out of the vehicle for some time. My son was so impacted by that experience, he was a changed boy.

I have come to expect amazing things from the Lord when He gives the burden of intercession. During worship one Sunday at church, we had a greeting time and I noticed a man in one of the back pews with his head down. Approaching him, I recognized him as someone who had called my husband for prayer a few weeks prior. I tried talking with him, but his responses were short and his grief obvious. His marriage was in serious trouble and he was carrying the burden of separation from his wife and children.

As I turned to walk away, the spirit of intercession hit me so strongly I began to weep with deep compassion. I knew something must happen with this burden of prayer from the Lord. Since he had called and asked for prayer in the past, I had authority to pray in this situation, to repent, and ask forgiveness. I was able to stand in the gap on his behalf. "I looked for a man among them who would build up the wall and stand before me in the gap on behalf of the land so I would not have to destroy it, but I found none." Ezek. 22:30.

Despite feeling a breakthrough at that moment, I didn't see this man again for several months, but I saw him again one Sunday at church. He and his wife and children were sitting in our usual spot when we walked in. They were beaming with love for one another and their joy glowed. I rejoiced at what God had done with this situation through a compassionate burden to pray.

Months later he phoned my husband and I took the call. I asked him if he remembered the day he visited our church and how I had approached him briefly during the greeting time.

"Oh yes! I sure do." He responded

"So what has happened in your life since then," I asked.

"About two weeks later my marriage came together and I was back with my family," he replied. "Since that time much of my life fell apart, but my family is now strong."

The burden of compassion in prayer always catches me off-guard and when I least expect it. Two young women stayed with us to help with a friend's wedding. One woman had an offence towards different members of my family for some years. I felt it, but didn't know how to deal with it. It became a major point of frustration for me, and at times felt I was in a battle that I would never win. She came into our home and everything seemed to be going well. Suddenly she exploded and violently expressed what was boiling inside of her. I questioned her but to no avail. She left.

Next morning someone called and asked me how the situation was. As we spoke the burden of prayer hit me and I began to weep.

"I have never prayed for this woman and her family like I need to pray now," I said.

My heart was breaking. I saw how the enemy was causing division and strife, destroying lives and causing turmoil. I felt the grief, compassion, and burden of the Lord for this situation.

But shortly after, I was touched to find those involved were walking in freedom they had never experienced. Overwhelmed, I rejoiced to see the power of the Holy Spirit, through prayer, set free those who were in bondage to the enemy. So many don't understand spiritual warfare and have no idea how the enemy works. In situations like this, we have responsibility to pray for their freedom.

On another occasion, my 81 year old mother-in-law contacted me by phone about her decision to take a trip to Holland to visit her family and friends for two weeks. The compassion prayer came upon me immediately. I saw this as an avenue for the Lord to get the gospel to these folk and for them to walk in the freedom of the Lord. Sensing the Holy Spirit on me, I spoke to her.

"I pray this time may be used to speak about what matters here on earth; that it will not be spent talking about the weather and people and every other thing. May you speak to them about the Lord and what God is doing."

I felt compassion for the bondage her family and friends were under, people that could be reached by my mother-in-law. I spoke this out as a prayer under the intense power of God on me.

I told my husband "Something is going to happen, and I cannot wait to hear the good news."

When my mother-in-law returned, we went to visit her, and she could not stop talking about what God had done. She told us how she talked with each person about the Lord and how Scripture came to her that she had forgotten. She was so excited that she didn't take naps and went to bed late without difficulty. The Lord gave her amazing strength in her body, her mind, and her spirit, to bring His word to the people in that country.

After leaving her home that night, I felt a strong burden to pray for her influence to be released by the Holy Spirit. She has many friends she visits frequently in a retirement home. The burden came that night, but the next morning, as I awoke, it flooded me so strongly, I shook. As I prayed I felt the strong power of God on me.

I told my husband, "Your mother needs to be used in that home for the glory of God."

She spoke to her dying sister in that home, and was used by God to hear her sister speak of her salvation and receiving the joy of the Lord before she died.

As we spend time in the secret place alone with God, we are empowered to go forth in love and compassion. Deep within His spirit, Jesus was in tune with the Father. This intimacy sent Him among the people to minister sensitively according to their needs. Jesus looked outside of Himself to see what others needed. We must do the same, through our actions and prayer.

We can make a difference in this world by walking compassionately in every area of our lives. If we plant seeds of mercy, people will notice and want what we have and will give the Lord opportunity to work in their lives. By this means, the kingdom of God will come to earth. Choose to be part of God's kingdom, joining an army of like-hearted, loving warriors who embrace the call to compassion.

CHAPTER 4

Knowing the Trinity

Our Christian life is to know God as Father, Son, and Holy Spirit, and have an individual, personal relationship with each Person of the Trinity. This will lead us to greater maturity, as Christ is coming back for His mature spotless Bride. He is calling us to a relationship of knowing the Father in the intimate way we know our earthly father—to have that child like trust a toddler has for his or her father.

He also calls us to know His Son, Jesus, as a bride knows the bridegroom; Jesus is the Bridegroom God coming back for His Bride. God desires us to have a deep relationship with the person of the Holy Spirit and have communion with Him. The Holy Spirit is the third person in the Trinity. He is not an entity, a force, or simply a source of power, but a person with whom we can have a personal relationship.

I thought I knew God, but something was missing. As the Lord spoke to me about the harvest and called me to prayer and compassion, I did not really know how to give the compassion to which the Lord was calling me. I continued to pray for the Lord to show me by whatever means how to walk in the "compassion of Christ." I knew I needed a full relationship with Jesus to receive that compassion, and once established, compassion would flow supernaturally.

Compassion is the very nature of Christ. The more we get to know Him, the more we are conformed into His image and will exhibit His compassion. Then I understood that it was not only about knowing

God, but rather a need for an intimate relationship with each individual Person of the Trinity.

Knowing the Father

> "I will be a Father to you, and you will be my sons and daughters," says the Lord Almighty. (2 Cor. 6:18)

The Father loves to take us by the hand and lead us in areas where we are weak. He wants our hearts and our commitment and He wants to give us the revelation of His Word. He loves to be approached and desires that we speak to Him as we would speak to our earthly father.

The Lord used the book, *The Purpose Driven Life,* by Rick Warren to bring me to a fuller understanding of God the Father. Two messages that spoke to my heart were entitled "Developing your friendship with God" and "Formed for God's Family." Warren writes:

Developing your friendship with God:

You are as close to God as you choose to be. Like any friendship, you must work at developing your friendship with God. It won't happen by accident. It takes desire, time, and energy. If you want a deeper, more intimate connection with God you must learn to honestly share your feelings with him, trust him when he asks you to do something, learn to care about what he cares about, and desire his friendship more than anything else.

Formed for God's Family:

When we place our faith in Christ, God becomes our Father, we become his children, other believers become our brothers and sisters, and the church becomes our spiritual family. The family of God includes all believers in the past, the present, and the future.

As I read these chapters, I learned a new concept of a father-daughter relationship. I began speaking to God as a child talking to a Father and His presence came over me. I felt His security, safety, and guidance as He stretched His loving hand to me and led me beside the quiet waters (Ps. 23:2). It opened a new door in my life where conversation between my Heavenly Father and I was effortless and became an important part of each day.

The freedom to see God as my Father was like a heavy cloud lifted from me. The Word became alive and began to illuminate what Jesus meant in Matthew 6:9: "This, then is how you should pray: 'Our Father in heaven, hallowed be your name . . .'" reminding us to address God as our Father.

I saw how the Word lifts up God as Father. As a Father He is described as "being worthy of praise" (Matt. 5:16), "perfect" (Matt. 5:48), "residing in heaven" (Matt. 6:1 and 23:9), and "wanting to give good gifts to those who ask" (Matt. 7:11). Mark also mentions, "offering forgiveness when we forgive" (Mark 11:25–26). As I gained a deeper realization of these truths, I built a deeper, more intimate relationship with God as Father.

This intimacy built my spirit. My husband and I went to visit his parents, and I tried to hold it all in, but felt about to burst. I walked into the kitchen with his mother and the love of the Father overwhelmed me so much, I wanted to shout, and I couldn't hold it in. Standing by the cupboard, I gazed up into the skylight above me; it seemed like gazing into my Father's face in Heaven. I had to proclaim the overwhelming love of the Father. My personal fears left and I spoke to her of the revelation that gripped me. She received it without negative response, and I knew a seed was sown.

All of God's fatherly attributes became so real to me that I exploded into the freedom to call God my Father. A completely new way to pray welled up within me. I felt a closeness to God I had never felt before, the intimacy of a father-daughter relationship and the protection that a father gives. I could not get enough. God wanted to give that to me, but not until I asked. "You have not because you ask not" (James 4:2). I asked to know God as my Father as I read that chapter by Rick Warren, and the Father's love enveloped me.

Jesus said, "Let the little children come to me, and do not hinder them, for the kingdom of heaven belongs to such as these." (Matt 19:14). Our Heavenly Father wants us to come as His little children.

Knowing the Son

> "You have stolen my heart, my sister, my bride, you have stolen my heart with one glance of your eyes . . . How delightful is your love, my sister, my bride! How much more pleasing is your love than wine . . ." (Song of Songs 4:9–10)

Jesus is the Son of God. He is the Bridegroom God, waiting for His bride to make herself ready. These are the words of Jesus wooing his bride to himself. The Song of Songs is an allegory of the love Christ has for His mature Church. As Jesus wooed me into His presence, calling me to come to His banqueting table, and revealing His banner of love over me, I was enthralled with the Bridegroom God, Jesus. I was faint with love.

Over the years He drew me into this intense relationship. It began one day as I spent time with two women I met in a class I had taken.

During a short conversation with these two women, one of them said, "You have a very strong relationship with the Father, and an amazing relationship with the Holy Spirit, but your relationship with the Son is minimal." As our conversation continued, the Holy Spirit gave these women insight as they unraveled what I was missing. It was clear the missing part in my journey was a relationship with Jesus.

The women asked if I had ever received Jesus as my personal Savior. I replied that I had in my heart, but had never spoken it out. They asked why. So I explained that I always understood that accepting Jesus in this way was a matter of "free will." But now I understood just speaking out that we accept Jesus is not salvation; we must make Him Lord of our life and have a relationship with Him.

I was overwhelmed with the revelation these women received. The only way I could receive the heart of compassion the Lord desired for me was through a relationship with Jesus. It couldn't be a true heart of compassion any other way. Right there, I repented for not understanding the concept of receiving and knowing Jesus in a personal relationship. This greatly enlightened me. I had no idea how wrong or missing concepts can hinder our walk with God to such a degree.

The next day I was visiting a special friend and explained this to her. We had been sitting at her table for more than an hour and a half when the phone rang. It had been silent our whole time together. As she looked at the call display, she responded in shock. "Janet, this is the Lord speaking," and I felt the Holy Spirit upon us. She turned the phone around for me to see. On the call display were the words: "Compassion Can."

She responded, "Compassion Canada has never phoned me in all my life!" We both sat there, our heads buzzing. It was such strong confirmation that the Lord was speaking. I had to leave, but the Holy Spirit continued to envelop me for some time.

This wooing began on January 13, 2010, but January 20, 2010 was a distinct day in my life. I was overcome by the love of Jesus our Bridegroom God. His presence was overwhelming and intense beyond words. He drew me into an intimate relationship with himself that brought me to the depth of the love that God has for His children. This testimony is explained later in this book in the section "Revelation of a Lovesick Bride of Christ—Our Created Purpose."

Transforming Into Compassion

Compassion is the very heart of Jesus. As we get to know Him and become transformed into His image, compassion will flow through us to others. "I want to know Christ and the power of his resurrection and the fellowship of sharing in his sufferings, becoming like him in his death . . ." (Phil. 3:10).

This transformation will come about as we get to know Him, and share in His suffering. We become purified as His spotless bride, and are made ready for His return. The Holy Spirit is sounding a clarion call to the Bride. That call is for us to walk in intimacy with the Lord Jesus Christ, our Bridegroom. This call is different from anything heard in previous generations or any other move of the Holy Spirit. As John the Baptist was a forerunner for Jesus' first coming, God is about to raise up a whole army of forerunners to prepare for the second coming of Christ.

They will proclaim the kingdom message—the Gospel of the Kingdom. "And this gospel of the kingdom will be preached in the whole world as a testimony to all nations, and then the end will come" (Matt 24:14). They will go throughout the whole world and preach the Gospel of the Kingdom; a testimony to all the nations.

Listen When He Calls

One morning as I sat down at the piano, the song open in front of me was, "I'll be Somewhere Listening." by V. O. Stamps. As I began to sing, I was overcome by the power of God and the presence of the Holy Spirit. I knew the Lord was calling me by my name.

> When the Savior calls I will answer, when He calls for me I will hear,
> When the Savior calls I will answer, I'll be somewhere list'ning for my name.
> If my heart is right when He calls me, If my heart is right I will hear,
> If my heart is right when He calls me, I'll be somewhere list'ning for my name.
> If my robe is white when He calls me, If my robe is white I will hear,
> If my robe is white when He calls me, I'll be somewhere list'ning for my name.

The Savior Jesus desires us to be listening when He calls. The presence of God was so strong I kept singing for about thirty minutes. I felt like a mess from weeping, hoping no one would come to the door. As I cleaned my face, ready to face the world, the door bell rang. I opened the door to a man who seemed very angry. I sensed evil spirits upon him but was eager to hear what he had to say. I had no fear; I was full of the presence of God. He asked if he could step inside and talk.

I said, "sure, come in."

In less than two minutes I saw the powers of evil leave this man and he changed, transformed to a most loving, soft, gentle nature, and gave me a courteous bow when he left.

I stood in front of the closed door and marveled at what had just taken place. I saw him freed in a couple of minutes. I saw the darkness leave, overtaken with light. One carried darkness and the other light. Light is stronger than darkness; we can walk in authority as we carry the light of Jesus. "You, dear children, are from God and have overcome them, because the one who is in you is greater than the one who is in the world" (1 John 4: 4).

Knowing the Holy Spirit

> May the grace of the Lord Jesus Christ, and the love of God, and the fellowship of the Holy Spirit be with you all. (2 Cor. 13:14)

To have fellowship with the Holy Spirit is to have companionship, friendly relationship, communion, to know Him in deep intimacy. I was twelve at my first encounter with the Holy Spirit. In church one Sunday, as we began to sing the last song of the service I was overcome by the presence of the Holy Spirit. It was a song from Psalm 132; a song of David finding a resting place for the Lord.". . . till I find a place for the Lord, a dwelling for the Mighty One of Jacob . . . arise, O Lord, and come to your resting place . . . For the Lord has chosen Zion, he has desired it for his dwelling."

The power of the Holy Spirit gripped me by this heavenly encounter. Weeping with a yearning deep within and not understanding the Holy Spirit, I tried to stop. I was embarrassed thinking everyone was watching me, but I only wept with more intensity as the congregation sang Psalter 367:

> Gracious Lord, remember David, how he made Thy house his care,
> How he vowed to seek no pleasure till Thy house he should prepare.
> Lord, remember his devotion; restless in his courts he trod
> Till he found a habitation fit for Israel's mighty God.
> Far away God's ark was resting; it is with His people now;
> We will go into His temple, at His footstool we will bow.
> With the ark Thy might revealing, enter, Lord, into Thy rest;
> Let Thy priests be clothed with justice, let Thy joyful saints be blest.
> Let the king behold Thy favor for Thy servant David's sake,
> Unto whom a sacred promise, Sure and faithful, Thou didst make.
> If his children keep Thy covenant and Thy testimony own,
> Then, as Thou, O Lord, hast promised, they shall sit upon his throne.
> Thou, the Lord, hast chosen Zion, Thou hast ever loved her well;
> This My resting-place forever, Here, Thou sayest, I choose to dwell.
> Surely I will bless and help her, feed her poor, her saints make glad,
> And her priests shall stand before Me in salvation's garments clad.
> I will cause the might of David ever more and more to grow,
> On the path of My Anointed I will make a lamp to glow;
> All His enemies shall perish, I will cover them with shame,
> But His crown shall ever flourish, blessed be His holy Name."

As a little girl it was hard for me to understand what the Holy Spirit was saying. Now I see the Lord marked me that day to be His Bride and to prepare to say "Come Lord Jesus"; to find a resting place for Him to dwell here. David was restless in the courts before the Lord until he found a habitation; a place to dwell—not a place to visit and leave, but a dwelling place fit for Israel's mighty God. The Lord is preparing His people to become the spotless Bride for His return, refined and made ready for the Bridegroom God. The question is: Are you ready?

I was completely overcome by the presence of God, weeping through that entire song, but not understanding the message. I was extremely shy and didn't ask anyone for insight. Now, forty years later, I know in part what the Holy Spirit was saying to me that day. The Father is marking the Bride for His Son and we must make ourselves ready, for the "Spirit and the Bride say 'Come'" (Rev. 22:17).

The cry of my heart is that we may all be aligned with God; that we may know and hear His voice. Is the Lord speaking to us and we do not know His voice?

Hearing the Holy Spirit

For some time I struggled with understanding God's voice. I wasn't sure how He spoke or whether He was speaking and not my own thoughts or imagination. Scripture says: "My sheep listen to my voice; I know them, and they follow me" (John 10:27). Surely, this meant that as one of His sheep I was capable of hearing His voice, listening to it, and learning to follow Him, but I questioned how this might happen much of the time.

As further confirmation that I was able to hear the voice of God, the Lord used a friend of ours. One day he walked through our kitchen and all he said was, "Ma'am, the Lord is going to speak to you tonight." My husband was out of town, and when he phoned later that evening I told him what had happened. We were both touched and left wondering what might happen. Once the house was quiet I sat to do some reading. As I read, I was sure to keep an open ear and to listen closely. While I read, "the fear of man brings a snare" (Proverbs 29:25), I wondered if that was God speaking, but I wasn't entirely sure.

Early the next morning my husband phoned me to ask if God had spoken to me.

"Maybe it was, I replied. 'The fear of man brings a snare', but I am not completely sure."

That morning, I took two of our children on a two hour drive. I sat in the backseat helping our son with his school work while our daughter drove. As we drove out of the yard I heard the verse again, "the fear of man brings a snare." A few minutes later I heard the same words again but a bit louder. For the rest of the drive I kept hearing the same words but louder. By the time we arrived at our destination the voice was so loud it seemed my ear drums would burst.

Eventually it was so loud all I wanted to do was plug my ears and scream. I screeched to the Lord saying, "Lord, please don't speak so loudly, next time I will listen when You speak softly!" The intensity of this lesson taught me to be extremely sensitive to His voice. Then I realized God had been speaking to me for some time, but I didn't know how to listen and hear from Him.

God's Love Poured Out

A marked moment in my life followed shortly after I began to understand hearing God's voice. While praying with two women on the phone, one of them stopped and began to weep uncontrollably. When she finally spoke, she said, "Janet, the Lord loves you so much. He is telling me, He loves you so much." She asked the other woman what she was sensing and she stated the same. One of the women suggested that I lay down and soak in the love of God.

I had never heard anything like this before, but that evening I did what I had been instructed to do. I wasn't sure where to begin, so I simply lay on my bed and began to pray, "Lord, here I am, to just lay here and soak in your love." Immediately, I felt the gentle love of God come upon me. It did not stop there, the next day it was a little stronger,

43

and the next stronger still. Each day I felt it reinforced increasingly. By day fourteen it was so strong I could not handle it. I wanted to scream and I felt I would explode. I simply cried out "Lord, why do You love me so much?" He immediately answered with a powerful voice, "Because you are radical with sin!"

Right then, the pressure released enough that I was able to get ready for a birthday party I was to attend. My husband was sick and I didn't want to go alone, so I invited our son to go. On the way I explained to him what I had just experienced, and why the power of God was so strong on us.

He responded, "Mother, I will never be the same."

I was not sure what touched him, and asked for an explanation.

"The part that you are radical in dealing with sin and God loves you so much for that, I will never forget," he answered. That moment made a very deep impression on him.

This is a key to being doused with the love of God. The Lord loves us to be radical against sin in our lives and not allow the sin of others to pull us down. As we pay the price, the Lord will bring us deeper into His presence. During this time, as the Holy Spirit revealed God's love to me, I also grew deeper in my knowledge of the Holy Spirit and His presence. When the Holy Spirit speaks to the heart, we will never be the same. The Lord brought me to a new level of understanding Him and walking in His presence. The Lord taught me the authority we have as we walk in His presence. As I got to know the Holy Spirit more intimately, I was amazed where He led me.

Authority

Peter called me a couple of minutes before a meeting he was to attend with several colleagues. He briefly told me it was a very dark meeting, saying: "It does not look good, it does not look good." I sensed his heavy discouragement, as though something terrible was about to happen. He told me he had contacted the top intercessor of another ministry and she could not even pray into this meeting without getting sick and vomiting. It seemed the spirit of death was there.

As my husband was on the phone explaining this, the power of God fell upon me. I ran for my coat and out the door on a prayer walk. I felt my prayers going higher and higher and myself going right into the throne room of heaven. I was standing before the Father at the throne. The throne was large and I felt so small. I could feel the power, authority, boldness and confidence of who I am in Christ driving me. I heard the Lord say, "I have given you the victory, because I have taken you into the *third heaven.*" I became confident of the breakthrough in the heavenlies.

My husband phoned me at the end of the meeting. "You will not believe what happened," he said. "The Holy Spirit came down and the people were sitting with their foreheads on the table, weeping."

I was puzzled by what it meant to be in the third heaven. Not having prayed for it, I wondered in amazement. I had won the victory because the Lord took me into the third heaven. The power of God on me was like riding a bulldozer, pushing through every force of the enemy, and reaching into the throne room. I saw myself standing before the throne in the presence of God.

> I know a man in Christ who fourteen years ago was caught up to the third heaven. Whether it was in the body or out of the body I do not know—God knows. And I know that this man—whether in the body or apart from the body I do not know, but God knows—was caught up to paradise. He heard inexpressible things, things that man is not permitted to tell. (2 Cor. 12:2–4)

It seemed the Lord had brought me to a new level of authority, but, I hasten to add, not comparing myself to the great apostle Paul.

The knowledge of the power of the Holy Spirit and the ability to walk in the authority God desires overwhelmed me. This is the work of the Holy Spirit that resides within us. The Lord has called me to share this so others can be encouraged and walk in this same authority. We need to know who we are in Christ and the authority we carry, it will change our lives.

CHAPTER 5

Being an Overcomer

As children of God, the Holy Spirit dwells within us and by Him we are overcomers. We overcome sin in our lives when we are in tune with the Holy Spirit. The Holy Spirit releases us from bondage; we are overcomers by the blood of the Lamb. When the Holy Spirit fills us, our yoke is easy and our burden is light (Matt. 11:30). "And his commands are not burdensome, for everyone born of God overcomes the world" (I John 5:3b–4a). We delight in His laws; they are not burdensome for the Holy Spirit gives us power to overcome. To be born of God is to be filled with the Holy Spirit. "And if anyone does not have the Spirit of Christ, he does not belong to Christ" (Rom. 8:9b). The Lord wanted me to understand this to the depth of my being.

One busy morning, I was rushing to get my work done, but noticed a little book lying by the side of my bathtub. The book gripped me in a way it never had before, despite having read it many times in the past. I didn't know why I was reading the book; I didn't have the time, but sat and read through to the end of the second chapter. I learned things completely new to me. This time I was learning with my heart, deep in my spirit, not just with my mind, as the Holy Spirit revealed truth.

The book was *The Christians Secret of a Happy Life*, by Hannah Whitall Smith. I understood for the first time that Christians "have power over sin, with the Holy Spirit." It was as thrilling as being on the highest mountain. I wanted to shout it to the whole world; I could hardly contain my excitement. I was set free from a bondage in my life by this truth revealed by the Holy Spirit. My eyes were unveiled as the Bible began to make more sense. Hannah writes:

> You have not lived as you feel children of God ought to live. You have had perhaps a clear understanding of doctrinal truths, but you have not come into possession of their life and power. You have rejoiced in your knowledge of the things revealed in the Scriptures, but have not had a living realization of the things themselves, consciously felt in the soul. Christ is believed in, talked about, and served, but He is not known as the soul's actual and very life, abiding there forever, and revealing Himself there continually in His beauty. You have found Jesus as your Savior from the penalty of sin, but you have not found Him as your Savior from its power. You have carefully studied the Holy Scriptures, and have gathered much precious truth therefrom, which you have trusted would feed and nourish your spiritual life, but in spite of it all, your souls are starving and dying within you, and you cry out in secret, again and again, for that bread and water of life which you see promised in the Scriptures to all believers. In the very depths of your hearts, you know that your experience is not a Scriptural experience; that, as an old writer said, your religion is "but a talk to what the early Christians enjoyed, possessed, and lived in." And your hearts have sunk within you, as, day after day, and year after year, your early visions of triumph have seemed to grow more and more dim, and you have been forced to settle down to the conviction, that the best you can expect from your religion is a life of alternate, failure and victory, one hour sinning, and the next repenting, and then beginning again, only to fail again, and again to repent.

> But is this all? Had the Lord Jesus only this in His mind when He laid down His precious life to deliver you from your sore and cruel bondage to sin? Did He propose to Himself only this partial deliverance? . . . Did "delivering us out of the hand of our enemies" mean that they should

still have dominion over us? Did "enabling us always to triumph" mean that we were only to triumph sometimes? Did being made "more than conquerors through Him that loved us" mean constant defeat and failures? Does being "saved to the uttermost" mean the meager salvation we see manifested among us now? Can we dream that the Savior, who was wounded for our transgressions and bruised for our iniquities, could possibly see of the travail of His soul and be satisfied in such Christian lives as fill the Church today? The Bible tells us that "for this purpose the Son of God was manifested, that he might destroy the works of the devil"; and can we imagine for a moment that this is beyond His power, and that He finds Himself unable to accomplish the thing He was manifested to do?

In the very outset, then, settle down on this one thing, that Jesus came to save you now, in this life, from the power and dominion of sin, and to make you more than conquerors through His power. If you doubt this, search your Bible, and collect together every announcement or declaration concerning the purposes and object of His death on the cross. You will be astonished to find how full they are. Everywhere and always, His work is said to be to deliver us from our sins, from our bondage, from our defilement; and not a hint is given, anywhere, that this deliverance was to be only the limited and partial one with which Christians so continually try to be satisfied.

This satisfied my deep hunger. The Holy Spirit gave this message to me. My spirit soared like an eagle. I rejoiced at a new understanding of the Word of God. The whole Bible came alive and I found life in the Word. I gained a new zeal to serve God; I came alive inside, something no one could take from me. I absorbed the Christian's secret of a happy life. The enemy does not want God's people to understand this secret because it reveals the power of the Holy Spirit within us. The Holy Spirit gives us power and authority, to deliver us from our enemies. They have no more dominion over us in the name of Jesus. We are empowered by His grace to do what truth demands of us.

Beware of False Teaching

The enemy tells us this teaching is "sinless perfection," a doctrine that claims we can become perfect and without sin. The word of God does not teach "sinless perfection." Victory in Christ isn't sinless perfection. That is a misunderstanding of the work of the Holy Spirit, denying His power. Be discerning when someone talks about the spirit, but not about the Holy Spirit. Only filled with the Holy Spirit do we have power to overcome:

> having a form of godliness but denying its power. Have nothing to do with them. They are the kind who worm their way into homes and gain control over weak-willed women, who are loaded down with sins and are swayed by all kinds of evil desires, always learning but never able to acknowledge the truth. (2 Tim 3:5–6)

Several women have come to me confused, thinking the book, *The Christian's Secret of a Happy Life,* teaches sinless perfection. Each time I heard this lie, the Holy Spirit came on me. At the first confrontation, the Holy Spirit was so strong I slept only minutes the entire night. Women, we need to have discernment, weigh everything with the Word and the Holy Spirit, especially for women today. We must not be weak-willed, loaded down with our sins, and swayed by all kinds of evil desires. We cannot be constantly learning but never able to acknowledge the truth (2 Tim. 3:7). We must become mature in handling the pure word of God.

Overcoming to Maturity

I asked the Lord what it means to be mature and how can we recognize it. The Lord opened Hebrews 5:14: "But solid food is for the mature, who by constant use have trained themselves to distinguish good from evil." We need to discern good from evil as the evil is all around us, often where we least expect it. The angel of light is impossible to discern without revelation from the Holy Spirit. Knowing good from evil is more than knowing there is a God and a devil. Walking with the Holy Spirit, in revelation and on guard, is the only source of distinguishing good from evil.

The enemy knows we women are the weaker vessel, and whispers deceit to lead us astray if we don't understand the truth of God's word. We are free from the bondage the enemy wants for us as we understand the secret to the happy life. It's all about being the overcomer. We are overcomers by the blood of the lamb and by the word of our testimony and we love not our lives even unto death (Rev. 12:11).

How can we overcome? What does it mean to be an overcomer? Only by the blood of the lamb and the indwelling Holy Spirit do we receive power and authority in the name of Jesus. Through the power of the Holy Spirit within us we can overcome and move mountains. Unstoppable, unmovable, unquenchable, greater is He that is in us than he that is in the world. As we discover what it means to overcome, the Word of God comes alive. John presents a duty: to overcome the evil one. "I write to you, young men, because you have overcome the evil one" (1 John 2:13b).

As I read the book of Revelation, I saw there many promises to the overcomer. "To him who overcomes, I will give the right to eat from the tree of life, which is in the paradise of God" (2:7). "He who overcomes will not be hurt at all by the second death" (2:11b). "To him who overcomes, I will give some of the hidden manna, I will also give him a white stone with a new name written on it, known only to him who receives it" (2:17b). I also noted the emphasis in 2:26: "To him who overcomes and does my will to the end, I will give authority over the nations . . ." The Lord is calling His people to be overcomers.

I read further. "He who overcomes will, like them, be dressed in white. I will never blot out his name from the book of life, but will acknowledge his name before my Father and his angels" (3:5). "Him who overcomes I will make a pillar in the temple of my God" (3:12). "To him who overcomes, I will give the right to sit with me on my throne" (3:21a). I could hardly imagine what this would be.

The promises to the overcomer are so overwhelming it is obvious why the enemy is trying to quench the Holy Spirit: to prevent us from becoming overcomers. We will not win the battle without the Holy Spirit. Through the truth of God's Word we can distinguish good from evil and be overcomers. We can only overcome evil as we discern good from evil. This is the call to maturity.

Knowledge of His Love

The Lord spoke to me with great power in two dimensions: "They overcame him by the blood of the Lamb and by the word of their testimony; they did not love their lives so much as to shrink from death" (Rev 12:11).

First, He gave me revelation of the "word of my testimony." I know the love, patience, faithfulness, wisdom, sovereignty, and all the attributes of God. The word of my testimony was "I know my God!" Excitement and fulfillment invaded my entire being. I understood that the God I pray to is all powerful, magnificent; His Name is above all names in heaven and on earth. This is the word of my testimony: knowing God, not just knowing about Him, but having an intimate, personal relationship with Him, seeing in Him all of His attributes.

"Those who know your name will trust in you" (Ps. 9:10 NIV). The Amplified Bible reads: "And they who know Your name (who have experience and acquaintance with Your mercy) will lean on and confidently put their trust in You." The word "name" means character, plus reputation. Why are there times when we do not have faith? After all, faith is simply confidence in the character of God? We will not have

51

faith if we do not know who God is; faith comes naturally when we learn who He is.

Living in the knowledge of who God is, there is nothing this world or the enemy can do to a Christian knowing the love of God, who swims in the ocean of His love as a small fish swims in a vast ocean. I felt protected by this truth.

Then, from the Lord, I understood, ". . . I love not my life even unto death" (Rev. 12:11 ASV). Nothing in this life had a grip on me, my love for God was stronger than death. Nothing and no one can compare to the love of God. It is deeper than any ocean and the seas cannot contain it. "That Christ may dwell in your hearts by faith; that ye, being rooted and grounded in love. May be able to comprehend with all saints what is the breadth, and length, and depth, and height . . ." (Eph 3:17–18 KJV). It is incomprehensible, indescribable, and impossible to understand without revelation from Him.

The Lord asked me clearly, "are you willing to walk off your property with the shirt on your back and trust Me?"

I responded without hesitation, "Yes, Lord."

We lived on a beautiful property in a large Victorian home surrounded with a white picket fence. There was a stately rock entrance, tall water fountain and coachman lights all around the property; a very peaceful setting. Yet this had no hold on me. Nothing that I possessed had any real meaning in my life because of the deep well of love I felt for God. This was later put to the test. We lost this beautiful property, and I faced the question from my friends,

"It must be hard to move off this beautiful property. How are you doing?"

I responded, "I have the call of the Bride of Christ. That is my passion, if I live here, or in town, or on the other side of the earth, it doesn't matter to me!"

My home there had no grip on me. This is only by the grace of God that I need for my life. Without that indwelling grace and passion for God I would have no strength to face each day.

Again, I heard the voice of the Lord ask, "are you willing to give your life for me?" I hesitated a couple of seconds before I could respond.

Then I yielded completely to Him, and immediately I knew "I loved not my life even unto death." This grace given by the Lord, is a special grace by the Holy Spirit which we need each moment. The Lord has called me to share my testimony of grace with you.

This grace is free and is waiting for us to receive it. "The grace of our Lord Jesus Christ be with you all" (2 Thess. 3:18). The Lord desires that all people draw on this grace. "Yet grace (God's unmerited favor) was given to each of us individually [not indiscriminately, but in different ways] in proportion to the measure of Christ's [rich and bounteous] gift" (Eph. 4:7 Amplified Version). There is freedom in knowing the gift of His grace He bestows on us. It is only by this grace that we can "love not our lives even unto death."

Call to Testimony

The Lord took me to the second dimension: "I'm an overcomer by the blood of the Lamb and the word of my testimony . . ." I realized the Lord was calling me to give my testimony of "who He is" to bring freedom to others. It has been astounding to see people understand who God is, what He does, and why He does things, by telling them where God has taken me. They better understood the Bible and God's ways by hearing my testimony. They have said: "a testimony makes the Word clear and I'll never forget what you explained. I don't always understand the Bible but your testimony makes it so clear."

Then I whisper a prayer, "Lord, please bless the words I have spoken." It is only by the Holy Spirit applying my words they will understand.

Our Testimony Dismantles Demons

What does a testimony do in the spirit realm? It overcomes the devil. "And they overcame him by the blood of the Lamb and by the word of their testimony" (Rev. 12:11). A testimony spoken by the Spirit of God has the power to dismantle demons. That's why we must allow the testing we go through to become our testimony. Satan does not want the events of our journey to become a testimony. The overcoming power of God's Spirit within us will displace the enemy and overthrow his strategy as we give testimony.

Our Call to Maturity

Understanding the stages of our lives and how to become an overcomer is shown in three stages. We become overcomers as we move into stage three. This is the stage of maturity.

The three stages to the Christian life are the convenience stage, the crisis stage, and the conviction stage. God uses trials, calamities, and afflictions to move us from the first (immature) stage to the third (mature) stage.

Stage One: The Convenience Stage—"Bless me Lord."

Everyone who comes to Christ begins at this stage. Unfortunately, many never move beyond this stage. The problem with Stage One Christianity is that our intimacy with God is limited. Our commitment to Him is determined by whether or not it is convenient for us to obey Him. Our faith is weak and elementary. God does not intend for us to remain at this primitive place in our relationship with Him.

Stage Two: The Crisis Stage—"Help me Lord."

There is something about a crisis that causes us to focus on God; it may be referred to as "foxhole Christianity." We can't remain at this stage. We must go deeper at this stage or we'll go back; people often go back to the previous stage. It is a tragedy to waste the lessons the Lord has for us.

When God sends a crisis into our life, He wants us to desire Him, to follow hard after Him, not just to seek Him to escape from the problem. The psalmist wrote, "My heart says of you, 'seek his face!' Your face, LORD, I will seek" (Ps. 27:8). God wants us to seek His face not just His hand; we tend to seek His hand of deliverance when we are in a crisis—an attitude of "Help me, Lord!"

God wants us to go deeper and further in our relationship with Him. But He wants us to go to the next stage to mature as His bride.

It is a time to focus on God with thanksgiving and praise in order to go to the next stage. If our focus remains on self we will not have the strength or grace to mature as the Lord has called us.

Stage Three: Conviction Stage—"Have me Lord."

God's desire is for us to develop an intimate and obedient relationship with Him—a relationship motivated by love. In this stage, our attitude is no longer "Bless me, Lord", or "Help me, Lord". At this point it is "Have me, Lord". The heart of the believer is fully circumcised at this stage and brought to obedience and humility. The believer is transformed and renewed; a new creation in Christ Jesus.

Job reached the conviction stage when he was able to say of God, "Though he slay me, yet will I hope in him" (Job 13:15). Through Job's trial, God accomplished that deeper work He desires to produce in our lives.

In the Conviction Stage, our focus is not on being saved, blessed or rescued. We begin to live the gospel of the Kingdom. We know who we are in Christ and we seek to glorify Him. We walk as Jesus walked. As we read in 1 John 2:5b–6: "This is how we know we are in him: Whoever claims to live in him must walk as Jesus did." This is God's desire for each of His children.

Walking in the conviction stage, we overcome and live the gospel of the Kingdom, and God produces the deeper work He seeks to accomplish in each of our lives. He desires us to develop in the Conviction Stage to bring us into full maturity as His Bride. A purifying takes place and we become more like Christ.

As overcomers we need perseverance: ". . . but he who stands firm to the end will be saved" (Matt. 24:13). This is the character of the overcomer. "Blessed is the man who perseveres under trial, because when he has stood the test, he will receive the crown of life that God has promised to those who love him" (Jas 1:12). The promises of God to the overcomer are rich, not only to us, but also to those who receive the word of our testimony.

"Watch your life and doctrine closely. Persevere in them, because if you do, you will save both yourself and your hearers" (1 Tim. 4:16). God's Spirit is the power source behind self-discipline so we can be an overcomer. We must discover that as Timothy did. For seven years I learned perseverance as I fought seven years to overcome the flesh. After winning that battle I faced conflict in the spirit realm. This battle also lasted seven years. Both of these struggles were very intense and nearly defeated me. But I was an overcomer by the blood of the Lamb.

We can only win the battle by the work of the Holy Spirit within. "I can do everything through Him who gives me strength" (Phil. 4:13). As I look back at what the Lord used to bring me to new levels of maturity through seven years of each battle, I understand that God's ways are perfect and right beyond our understanding. The number seven represents perfection and completion, a fulfillment of the will of God.

Struggle to Victory

After the fourteen years of winning the struggle to overcome, I knew I had entered a new season. In the year 2010 I felt I was entering a season of intimacy with Jesus, operating out of the resting place. "There is a time for everything, and a season for every activity under heaven . . ." (Eccl. 3:1). During the seven years of refining my life in the flesh I gained strength in the Lord, my only hope in those years of desperation. God used those years to reveal what was in my heart and provide strength to endure the spiritual battle to follow. I learned much about God's heart and the importance of perseverance.

Scripture records how Hezekiah and Moses were tested to know their heart.

> God withdrew from Hezekiah in order to test him and to see what was really in his heart. (2 Chron. 32:31)

> Remember how the Lord God led you all the way in the desert these forty years, to humble you and to test you in order to know what was in your heart, whether or not you would keep his commands. He humbled you, causing you to hunger and then feeding you with manna, which neither you nor your fathers had known, to teach you that man does

not live on bread alone but on every word that comes from
the mouth of the Lord. (Deut. 8:2–3)

During this time of darkness reading the Bible left me feeling
condemned. I slept only twenty minutes during eight days and nights,
so Scriptures like, "when you lie down, your sleep will be sweet" (Prov.
3:24) and "He grants sleep to those He loves" (Ps. 127:2) left me feeling
condemned; I could not possibly be considered one of "those He loves."

During this season I did not understand that I was going into
depression. By nature, I am a happy woman and I was caught off
guard. One day most of my hair fell out and I had to wear a wig, it
was devastating. I had never experienced depression and it came on
so quickly and with such severity I had no idea how to combat it. It
seemed like a losing battle I was totally unprepared for. As a result I
went into complete denial. I didn't know who to talk to and I didn't
want anyone to know what I was going through. Therefore, I began
living one day, even one moment at a time, anxious for the days to pass.
This was my dark night of the soul, nothing made sense to me and the
heavens seemed brass. The Lord humbled me through this, causing me
to hunger for Him.

After a couple of years I began to recover, but then went into a
backward spiral that got worse at an alarming rate. At this point I knew
I had to get a grip fast if I was going to recover. At night, as soon as
my husband was asleep, I decided I would go into another room and
pray. During these times my mind was in a strong intentional focus on
others; I knew one moment thinking of myself and my problem would
bring me into utter despondency. So I would not pray for myself to
avoid despair, but instead I would pray for our children's salvation and
for my father's healing, among other things. This began to assure me of
my own salvation, since I was struggling with my identity as a child of
God. Even in the darkness I was experiencing, some life came back to
me. I began to feel the heart of God and started to understand spiritual
warfare and intercession on a personal level.

Praying for others was my first step towards victory in this battle. I
knew I was recovering slowly as my focus was not on me and I prayed

desperately for others, crying out for their needs through many night hours.

Many years later, reading the book of Job, I read his testimony how praying for others changed his life. "After Job had prayed for his friends, the Lord made him prosperous again and gave him twice as much as he had before" (Job 42:10).

Oswald Chambers has a beautiful devotional in his book, *My Utmost for His Highest,* where he expounds this verse. In the last part of the message he writes:

> If you are not now receiving the "hundredfold" which Jesus promised (see Matt. 19:29), and not getting insight into God's Word, then start praying for your friends—enter into the ministry of the inner life. "The Lord restored Job's losses when he prayed for his friends." As a saved soul, the real business of your life is intercessory prayer. Whatever circumstances God may place you in, always pray immediately that His atonement may be recognized and as fully understood in the lives of others as it has been in yours. Pray for your friends now, and pray for those with whom you come in contact now.

This again emphasized what I had walked through and the power of this message.

Desperate for God

Despite being diagnosed "manic depressed," I decided I hadn't been born this way and I would not live this way. A fight rose up within me. I knew it would be a long, hard battle, and I knew my strength would not carry me through. My focus became desperate for God. I asked Peter every few months:

"Am I back to normal yet?"

At the end of the seventh year he said, "Yes, you are now your normal self! I'm so glad to have you back!"

It was a long time but the Lord knew what He was doing. I learned to draw on God's grace and to be dependent on Him in my weakness. Without His strength it would have been even impossible to get out of bed each morning. I really know my weakness and the power of Christ to sustain and the grace of God to endure. As Paul states: "Therefore I will boast all the more gladly about my weaknesses, so that Christ's power may rest on me" (2 Cor. 12:9).

It was impossible for me to see the process I needed to go through to overcome during this season. As when a caterpillar becomes a butterfly, each stage is critical. If you break the caterpillar from the cocoon stage, it will never have the strength to fly. Premature release from any stage in this process would have been detrimental for me. Although it seemed difficult at the time, God knew what I could handle and acted accordingly. This is also a Biblical concept: "No discipline seems pleasant at the time, but painful. Later on, however, it produces a harvest of righteousness and peace for those who have been trained by it" (Heb. 12:11).

This was a time of despair. My hope was dim. One day a man approached Peter to tell him to prepare to take me to the hospital monthly and possibly bi-weekly. Another man approached him and said, "this is what powerful women of God are made of!" I had no concept of what he meant with this statement, but it spoke life into my spirit and I held onto it, even though I didn't understand it.

I struggled with self worth. I felt my children did not have a mother and it crushed my spirit. Arising one afternoon, knowing two of our children were home I found them sitting on a small bed in the furnace room. Our ten year old daughter was rocking our two year old son in her arms trying to give him the mother love that a small child needs. I could only turn around and weep in grief. My children needed me and I had no strength in my body, mind, or spirit to go on. I returned to my room despondent. Would it ever be possible to recover and enjoy life with my family again? I hoped for what seemed impossible.

As I was praying for others the next stage in the process was for me to see the reality of God through answers to my prayers. The book of Romans tells us to be ". . . patient in affliction, faithful in prayer"

(Romans 12:12). When I became desperate and turned to God in prayer He began to move. My daughters came forward to be baptized. Seeing prayers answered, I began praying with faith instead of desperation. Until then, I had only used prayer to keep my mind in control, as I did when I gave birth to each of my children.

I was taught in the prenatal classes before our first child was born, to use counting during giving birth to our children to keep my mind in control. Otherwise, I would have gone screaming out of control. This was my intent as I lay, not able to sleep for many hours, for up to eight days in a row. My focus on prayer for others kept my mind stable. I would pray through the night and get up and go as if I had slept. My family could not tell I was not sleeping. My prayer time for others was reviving my spirit giving my body and mind strength. I marvel at the power of prayer. It became the life within me. I could not tell then if God was even there, but I had nothing to lose and could have everything to gain.

Next, I saw my father receive healing. For the first time I was seeing the power of prayer firsthand, God was hearing me and a new level of faith arose within. Over time God set me free and healed me from the depression as well as the anti-depressants and tranquillizers I had been taking.

Spirit Warfare

Four days after my husband gave me words of encouragement saying that I was back to my normal self, I faced forces of evil that caused deep turmoil in my spirit. This was the beginning of the seven year battle in the spirit. The Lord revealed to me this was not a battle in the flesh but in the heavenlies. As Job saw the battle with God and Satan (Job 1: 8), my battle was between the demonic world and the Holy Spirit. "For our struggle is not against flesh and blood, but against the rulers, against the authorities, against the powers of this dark world and against the spiritual forces of evil in the heavenly realms" (Eph. 6:12).

As I sensed this in my spirit, I knew it explained what I discerned. The Lord wanted me to comprehend walking in the Spirit, coming against the forces of evil and overcoming the enemy. For a long while, Romans chapter 8 became a favorite for understanding life through the Spirit. The Lord wanted me grounded in that truth. I dwelt on verses 9 to 14, "and if anyone does not have the Spirit of Christ, he does not belong to Christ . . . because those who are led by the Spirit of God are sons of God."

My first encounter with the demonic realm caught me unaware. It was a busy morning, my husband was on a trip with his business partner, and it was our son's birthday. My husband called and asked me to pray but provided no details. I began to pray for him and his partner. I did not realize his battle was an encounter with the demons along the Florida coast. I instantly felt them coming up to me as a wall which came to within two inches of my nose. I felt supernatural power come upon me as I encountered them, pressing them down and back as I prayed. I knew I had authority over them in the name of Jesus. I had no fear but felt complete authority through His name. "I have given you authority to trample on snakes and scorpions and to overcome all the power of the enemy; nothing will harm you" (Luke 10:19).

The entire day I felt a continual flow of the Holy Spirit on me as if I was walking several inches above the ground. The power of prayer was clearly evident to us through this encounter with the spirit realm. The two men returned with such excitement. My husband's partner stated, "A movie must be made of what we experienced!" He was shocked and amazed and felt the world needed to know who God is and how He answered our prayers.

Facing the realm of evil, I knew that I had much to learn. I marveled how God continually sent the right person to guide and direct me, and speak words of encouragement with prophetic messages.

One year I could not walk into a meeting place without having someone approach me with a prophetic word. People I had never met would come to me with words that coincided; much the same word spoken differently. Prophecy is given for encouragement and I would not have been able to walk through that year without it. The Lord knew

I was not strong alone so He sent His people around me, as the body makes us complete. I realized how important each part of the body is; each part is significant. The hand cannot say to the foot, I have no need of you.

I marveled at the people the Lord brought across my path at unexpected times and unexpected places; about twenty five people the first year. Much of the message was regarding going to the nations, traveling the world, taking down witchcraft and demonic forces. It was over my head and I felt inundated, but witnessed the immense grace God gave to overcome the forces of the evil one. The enemy tries to abort the work of God before it is born and I saw how the doctors and nurses in the Spirit came around me to carry me through.

I knew very little about prophecy before that time. But what do you do when people come up to you, people you have never met and they start giving you words from the Lord? It was then that I understood that we must not despise prophecy, but covet the gift of prophecy—the only thing the entire word of God tells us to "covet" (1 Cor. 14:39). Then I knew how we need the revelation of God's Word, and its truth. If we have not received the full revelation in the past, we only need to seek out more truth. God is so good and He is gracious, He wants to teach His children, and He graciously taught me, many times by bringing others around me.

Two women came along side me during this time and said the Lord had spoken to them to walk with me; one had received a message to pray with me weekly. They were sent to me by God to teach me spiritual warfare and guide me through the journey to which the Lord was drawing me. This was all so foreign to me, I was overwhelmed. Both these women were anointed in the prophetic, receiving revelation about what I faced. My husband introduced them to me because he had such great respect for them. He wanted me to pray with them because he sensed their anointing but did not know what it was. He knew they were genuine because without knowing him they unraveled things in his life; they had to be hearing from God. So I began praying each week with them; one by phone and the other lived close and we were able to spend time together.

CHAPTER 6

Thanksgiving and Praise

The key that unlocks the gates of heaven is a thankful heart; we enter the courts of God as we begin to praise the Lord. A thankful man is a humble man. Of course, it may be false humility which we address later in this book.

"Pride slays thanksgiving . . . . a proud man is seldom a grateful man, for he never thinks he gets as much as he deserves." H.W. Beecher

Thanksgiving is an appropriate response to God's grace in our lives. Notice the instruction in 1 Thessalonians 5:18: "give thanks in all circumstances, for this is God's will for you in Christ Jesus." We are to give thanks "in" the midst of whatever is happening, not "for" everything that happens.

It is the Word of God that sets us free and thanksgiving uplifts the power of that Word in our lives. This motivates our faith and prepares us for the miracle working power of God. God is also overjoyed with thanksgiving that acknowledges His answers to our prayers.

Heartfelt Thanksgiving

Traveling with my daughter one late evening I had fallen asleep by 2 a.m. We had booked a hotel hours further down the road than what we had anticipated. She had stopped at a gas station and filled up and left her clutch purse on the roof of the car. It had not dawned on her until nearly 30 minutes later. She was missing her purse with all her identification, money, credit cards and even her cards for entrance into the university.

She panicked! Shocked she said, "Mother, I don't have my purse! What can I do?" I immediately woke, sat up and tried to decide what was best at this late hour. How would we ever find this little purse again? It would be a miracle. We decided to continue driving to the hotel we had booked, still a further hour away.

Soon after sunrise we made our way back to the gas station. My daughter approached the attendant, but he had no recollection of her purse. I stepped into the washroom while my daughter went immediately to the roadside ditches. As I stepped outside I saw several people helping my daughter find her purse. I chuckled inside thinking, "this is just like my daughter, she so easily pulls people together. She has a way with people!"

Back at the car I put on my running shoes, my daughter came running with her purse in her hand raised as high as she could reach.

She yelled out "we found it, we found it!"

I sat with my mouth open in shock.

She went on. "This man you sent out found it! Mother, it is just like you, you so easily pull people together. You have a way with people!"

"What?" I exclaimed, "I did nothing! I thought you pulled this together, it was nothing I did; this was the Lord!"

As I began to drive, my heart went out with such thanksgiving to the Lord, I was bursting. Instantly I felt the presence of God upon me; it was so irresistible I wept deeply. He was so pleased with the overwhelming sense of gratitude. I felt the kisses of God. The Lord loves us as His beloved . . . . I am my Beloved's and His desire is toward me.

Praise

A relationship with God cannot exist without praise. Thanksgiving responds to what God has done, while praise relates to who God is. This distinction is not absolute, but it is a good guide. We can understand the Psalms in that light. Psalms of descriptive praise, and Psalms of declarative praise. The Psalms of declarative praise have an emphasis on what God has done for His people, which declares the glory of God. Thanksgiving relates to the Psalms of declarative praise.

Psalms of descriptive praise exult in the person of God, His attributes, all about who He is. Psalm 138:1 says: "I will give Thee thanks with all my heart; I will sing praises to Thee before the gods" (NASB)

Praise is a powerful weapon against the Devil. It silences him. Praise will bring the weapons of God to bear against the attacks of the Evil One.

Testimony of Praise and Worship

There are many testimonies I could share about the power of praise. My phone rang one afternoon. A man called to tell me he was spending time in prayer when the Lord told him he needed to give me a message. I had just returned home from the hospital after three days of antibiotic intravenous. The doctor who released me stated, "We have no idea what was happening with you, your white blood count was over 24 thousand and now it is normal. You can go, but it is a mystery." I was still feeling weak and sickly, not completely able to do my usual duties.

This man called and gave me this message, "Janet, you have the spirit of infirmity on you, the enemy wants you to be weak and sickly. The only way you will combat the enemy and regain your strength is through praise and worship. You must get behind your piano and play and worship till it breaks." After two hours of basking in the presence of God, it broke and I was back to normal.

Days later my husband and I attended a conference where Chuck Pierce was speaking. In his message he stated, "The enemy is coming on the people of God with the spirit of infirmity to keep them weak and sickly. The only way you will combat this is through praise and worship." We marveled and knew God was speaking a second time to confirm.

I pray this testimony will help others understand the amazing power there is in praise and praise with worship to combat the power of the enemy in our lives.

PART II:
Secrets of the Kingdom Revealed

CHAPTER 7

The Power of Suffering

For we who are alive are always being given over to death for Jesus' sake, so that his life may be revealed in our mortal body. So then, death is at work in us, but life is at work in you. (2 Cor. 4: 11–12)

The Word of God is powerful, sharper than any two edged sword, cutting between soul and spirit. The above text cut between my soul and spirit; the Spirit of God made it real to me, for the Holy Spirit brings the word alive. We can read the Scriptures over and over and they seem like a mystery or a dark saying; we read it with a veil over our understanding. It is not clear, but what can we do about it? It seems beyond us. We go on reading, thinking because God is so much greater than us we will never understand what He is saying. But He wants us to understand His Word. As the Holy Spirit illumines a portion, then the rest of the Bible begins to make more sense.

This happened to me. I saw the "power of suffering" as this revelation unfolded. Every person goes through suffering at some time in their lives, both those that know the Lord and those that do not. If we yield to God's plan for Christ to be formed in us, God will use our sorrows and sufferings to enlarge our hearts. Once we have been acquainted with grief and suffering, we then can be anointed with compassion to deliver others.

Suffering comes in various places: health, marriage, finances, unruly children, relationships, or the work place. We are responsible to respond to suffering with a heart that understands God's Word. Walking through the three aspects of revelation I had received, I was overjoyed at what God wants His children to understand. Our response to suffering gripped me as I understood that God's Word produces life! The more we die, the more we bring life to others.

Other versions of the Bible helped me gain a deeper grasp on this message. The Amplified reads, "Thus death is actively at work in us, but (it is in order that our) life (may be actively at work) in you." I saw more as I read the NAS, "So death works in us, but life in you." Then more in the NKJV, "So we live in the face of death, but it has resulted in eternal life for you."

I searched to understand suffering and what takes place when we overcome. We choose how we handle the suffering we encounter. We suffer with repentance, with a heart after God. We don't think, *poor me, I've been hurt, I'm suffering*, or focus on ourselves; perhaps to get attention and comfort from others.

This is a matter of light and darkness, a matter of releasing life or releasing death. "Godly sorrow brings repentance that leads to salvation and leaves no regret, but worldly sorrow brings death" (2 Cor. 7:10). For further clarity I went to the NLT which reads: "For God can use sorrow in our lives to help us turn away from sin and seek salvation. We will never regret that kind of sorrow. But sorrow without repentance is the kind that results in death." The Amplified Bible also provides a clear explanation:

> For godly grief and the pain God is permitted to direct, produce a repentance that leads and contributes to salvation and deliverance from evil, and it never brings regret; but worldly grief (the hopeless sorrow that is characteristic of the pagan world) is deadly—breeding and ending in death.

God has not promised to keep us from suffering, but He has promised to make us fruitful in it as we follow Him. The character and nature of Christ will emerge in our spirits as we remain faithful to Him in trials, and releases the life within us to others. Our life will be a key that unlocks God's stronghold to others. This is where we graduate into the power of God.

Everyone faces suffering in their lives, and we have a choice to make. We can either become bitter or we can become better. God may allow suffering in our lives for a number of reasons. We see in the book of Job God's perspective on adversity. We can see Job's journey and how it can apply to our lives. The number of reasons might be: "to test us (2:3), to discipline us (5:17), to humble us (22:29), to change our perspective (42: 5–6), or to prepare us for future blessings (42:10)."

The Lord takes us through the test of suffering to purify us, and it also releases the Holy Spirit on others as He fills us in greater measure. This truth is rich, and God will use it to bring glory to cover our land The Lord revealed this to me many times as I walked in His presence. He desires all His people to walk this out increasingly. One of the keys is a proper response to suffering; to become like Jesus in the midst of our test.

We are blessed as the Lord uses adversity to discipline us, and we must not despise His discipline. Discipline purifies and as we respond with repentance we release life, the fragrance of Christ. Even as He humbles us with adversity, He loves our response of submission to Him. I learned to walk in repentance, to glorify God from my heart, careful not to quench the Holy Spirit.

The message of the "power of suffering" is for every person. It struck me even harder for those that have been enlightened. What will the Day of Judgment be for those that have known this way, have walked in repentance and lived in the presence of the Holy Spirit, and then fallen away?

> It is impossible for those who have once been enlightened, who have tasted the heavenly gift, who have shared in the Holy Spirit, who have tasted the goodness of the word of God and the powers of the coming age, if they fall away, to be brought back to repentance, because to their loss they are

crucifying the Son of God all over again and subjecting him
to public disgrace. (Heb. 6:4–6)

We can learn more from God's word on this topic from Ezekiel:

"But if a righteous man turns from his righteousness and
commits sin and does the same detestable things the wicked
man does, will he live? None of the righteous things he has
done will be remembered. Because of the unfaithfulness he
is guilty of and because of the sins he has committed, he will
die." (Ezek. 18:24)

I didn't think it possible for a man to fall away once he was saved
until I read the stirring book by John Bevere, *Driven by Eternity*. I
couldn't put the book down once I began reading. My spirit was so
stirred I told my husband, "Every person needs to read this book." As
the word became clearer, I noted 1 Timothy. 4:1: "The Spirit clearly says
that in later times some will abandon the faith and follow deceiving
spirits and things taught by demons." This is surely a warning to us to
walk in repentance and not focus on ourselves and our adversity. We
will study suffering in three parts as the Word of God teaches: only as
we reflect His image, glory released, and we release life.

Only as We Reflect His Image

Called to maturity we will reflect His image. The more we know
Jesus the more we will imitate Him. Being born again is just the
beginning of God's work in us. Ninety-nine percent is yet to be done.
We have excitement and joy over our salvation, but we soon discover
God is not yet satisfied with what we are.

God did not create man just to tend His garden, and He did not save
us simply to have workers for His harvest field. God's original and sole
purpose for man has always been to manifest His image from intimacy

with Him. That's what He desires when He begins to deal seriously with our human nature.

We are confident at first perhaps, thinking He can complete this job in no time, because we don't think we are so bad. But He shows His true image in many Scriptures like these:

> For this is what the high and lofty One says—He who lives forever, whose name is holy: "I live in a high and holy place, but also with him who is contrite and lowly in spirit, to revive the spirit of the lowly and to revive the heart of the contrite." (Is. 57:15)

> "Has not my hand made all these things, and so they came into being?" declares the Lord. "This is the one I esteem: he who is humble and contrite in spirit, and trembles at my word." (Is. 66:2)

The deep humility and total submission of Jesus is what God desires for each of His children. But, how can we ever become like this when we see our very nature is proud, selfish, and stubborn? Our world has taught us from birth that we have rights and we must fight for them. We need to be ambitious and unbending; and to value success, ability, and position above everything else.

Not Able People, But Broken People

The Bible teaches us God is indeed able to change us into His likeness, but only through one way: the process of brokenness. God works in our lives, breaking us, changing us, purifying us, and putting to death our selfish desires, until His nature shines through.

How important is brokenness for our service in God's Kingdom? Can God use us outside of brokenness? A.W. Tozer once said that he doubted God could ever use a man until He had broken him thoroughly and empowered him.

I read of a missionary leader who was looking for a teacher for his seminary. He was asked for his opinion on a highly educated candidate. He said, "As far as academics are concerned, he would be one of the greatest assets we could have in our school. We could not find a more intellectual man or one so incredibly gifted and able to communicate.

"However, his coming would be dangerous and disastrous for our institution. The reason is simply this: you know as much as I do that this man is not broken. He is so self-sufficient, strong, and sure of himself. If there is an argument, he always wins. In a group, he acts important so he will be noticed.

"He has been to many places, but he's never remained anywhere. It's not because he's not able; it's due to lack of humility. Even if he gave us thousands of dollars and begged us to allow him to teach, I would never allow it. If he were at the seminary, he would produce unbroken, stubborn students just like himself. God is not looking for able people, but for broken people."

God's greatest concern is our brokenness. We can only reproduce what we are ourselves. Only through brokenness can we experience resurrection life and rivers of living waters flowing unhindered from our innermost being.

We can be very gifted, but if we are not broken, we cannot be used for God's glory. "For those God foreknew he also predestined to be conformed to the likeness of his Son, that he might be the firstborn among many brothers" (Rom. 8:29). "And we, who with unveiled faces all reflect the Lord's glory, are being transformed into his likeness with ever increasing glory, which comes from the Lord, who is the Spirit" (2 Cor. 3:18).

Isn't God's word rich? This transforming can only come by the Spirit. Man can't do any of this on his own, it is by the power of the Holy Spirit within us who renews us day by day. We are to have the mind of Christ.

Glory Released

God is releasing His glorious presence upon His people; upon those that know suffering and are overcoming it with their focus on Christ and His perfected work on the cross; those with eyes of adoration on their risen Savior and Lord, suffering for His name's sake; those whose desire is for God's glory and the glory of His kingdom.

God does not look for perfection, He wants our hearts. He wants a heart searching for purity, brokenness and humility. I sensed how much He loved me even though I saw myself undone, trying, but failing, alone and misunderstood. He saw my obedience to serve Him and my heart sold out to His service. His love overwhelmed me. I write this to encourage those who want to be overcomers and yet find it difficult to pay the price. God is there when we need Him. He loves us when we don't feel loved. He sees and hears us in our darkest hour.

"YOU are approved of God, you ARE approved of God, you are APPROVED of God, you are approved of GOD, YOU ARE APPROVED OF GOD!" As the pastor came to the pulpit and turned to face the people I saw the glory come down on his head. In the instant he spoke these words and as the speed of sound, I felt, as it were, a heat seeking missile carrying those words hit my chest. It looked like an 18 inch cylinder coming towards me with those words; I knew it was the glory of God. I immediately collapsed and fell groaning in the magnificent presence of God.

When this happened, I was standing in the presence of God feeling completely spiritually numb. I considered I had done everything wrong and felt condemnation tempting me. The Lord saw me completely overcome with weakness with no strength to carry on. I had never come to that point in my life before. In His love and compassion He revealed Himself to me in a way I could never doubt He was with me and loved me. He opened His pleasure towards me. I felt the love of God being released as Jesus did at His baptism, when God spoke from heaven, "This is my beloved son of whom I am well pleased."

"But rejoice that you participate in the sufferings of Christ, so that you may be overjoyed when his glory is revealed" (1 Pet. 4: 13). I could only rejoice because He revealed His glory to me. When I explained this to an intercessor friend the next day, she suggested I put banners throughout my home with "I am approved of God," to let the words penetrate into my spirit so I would walk in confidence.

Approved of God

"Do your best to present yourself to God as one approved, a workman who does not need to be ashamed and who correctly handles the word of truth" (2 Tim. 2:15). The Lord was telling me not to be ashamed as I correctly handle the word of truth, a workman approved of God. When the Lord speaks we can only melt under His power as I did that day. When we are aligned with God, we are in position to receive his glory. But if we are not so aligned, we are in danger of his displeasure.

What does it mean to share in his glory? We read in Romans 8:17, "Now if we are children, then we are heirs—heirs of God and co-heirs with Christ, if indeed we share in his sufferings in order that we may also share in his glory." In fact, our experience of suffering works in us a glory "beyond all measure" (2 Cor. 4:17, NRSV). Paul connects our present "light" and "momentary" suffering with the "eternal weight of glory." But the measure of glory always outweighs the measure of suffering; that is the good news. But the fact remains—no suffering, no glory. There is a process. Our response to suffering is the key.

So the weight of the coming visitation will be measured against our suffering. How does this work? If we co-operate with Him in times of suffering, the Holy Spirit will create within us three conditions of heart: purity, brokenness, and humility. The refining process is taking place.

I stood in God's house sharing in His suffering, to the point that my body felt numb with warfare, greater than I had ever felt. There I *saw* the glory of God. And I felt the glory of God hit me with power. I realized later, I saw His glory because of my suffering. That was not the only reason, but it came with the message of "you are approved of God!" I also realized later I was suffering for the name of Christ which brought about the intense glory of God. The Lord led me to Romans 8:17 to show me we can share in His glory.

The Lord is measuring us to determine how much of His glory we desire. Are we ready to make our shift and jump into God's river? The river in Ezekiel represents God's glory.

> The man brought me back to the entrance of the temple, and I saw water coming out from under the threshold of the temple toward the east (for the temple faced east). The water was coming down from under the south side of the temple, south of the altar. He then brought me out through the north gate and led me around the outside to the outer gate facing east, and the water was flowing from the south side . . . He measured off another thousand, but now it was a river that I could not cross, because the water had risen and was deep enough to swim in—a river that no one could cross. (Ezek. 47:1–5)

We are empowered and positioned for entrance into His glory in His secret place. Here He empowers us to move from one level of glory to another.

We Release Life

Why do the children of God suffer? Shouldn't we, who give our lives to Jesus and receive Him as Savior and Lord, escape the suffering that we see in the world around us? God is a God of love, He loves us so much that surely He would care for us so we would live as His child; covered with great wealth and know nothing that would cause us heart ache, grief, or sorrow.

This is what our rational mind would say to us; it seems logical outside of the teaching of God's Word. But it is through the Word that we receive truth.

While suffering with repentance and a heart of love toward God, our prayer is "Have me Lord, I am yours, I trust you with everything

I am and have. Only You matter in my life." Eternal life flows through us and is released to others.

We are increasingly made into His image, and transformed by the renewing of our minds. Suffering releases the glory of God on us, enabling us to release life to others. As recipients of the indwelling Holy Spirit, we release the fragrance of Christ. Living in the face of death results in eternal life being released to others; it is life at work, released by the Holy Spirit. This produces the spotless Bride for whom Jesus is coming back. We cannot become the spotless Bride without it. This is what transforms us into His likeness.

Being Aware

I became aware of the release of the Holy Spirit one Sunday. Peter and I were at the front of the church to pray for those who had come forward with needs. I asked one lady what she would like me to pray for.

"I believe I have a high call from God on my life," she said, "but I feel the enemy overtaking me. I need to be anointed with oil."

I knelt down beside her, my arm around her shoulders.

"Let's do that together," I suggested.

I opened a small phial of olive oil from my purse. "This anointing oil won't do anything, but it is a symbol of the Spirit's anointing that we seek." I touched some on her forehead.

She nodded, and I prayed with her. I prayed the Holy Spirit would release her from the sense of bondage she felt, especially from the evil spirits who were likely oppressing her.

As we finished praying, she burst out joyfully: "I felt the Holy Spirit on you released to me. The forces of the enemy fled. I heard the last one saying as he left, 'I must go, I cannot stay here any longer."

I explained to her. "As I prayed, I felt the Holy Spirit come on me and be released on you. You have confirmed what happened. With that authority every demonic force has to go. Remember God's word? 'Greater is He that is in us than he that is in the world.'"

She was so excited. She had been set free from the forces of the enemy, and went on her way rejoicing. This confirmed to me the teaching of the Word of God.

Releasing His Fragrance

A few months later, we were meeting with a man to discuss a matter, when my husband received a call and had to leave. Our conversation flowed into testimonies of God's presence.

"We haven't seen one another for maybe a couple of years," I began. "Let me tell you some happenings since then." He had spent time in our home in earlier years and had spoken into our lives many times.

I went on. "The Lord led me into a profound experience of seeing His glory." He raised his eyebrows in surprised interest. "Yes! It was a Sunday morning in church and I saw and felt His glory. That glory hit me in my stomach. At the time I was so empty, I hardly felt alive."

He listened intently, his eyes like saucers, drinking in every word and each expression. It felt I was reliving the moment it happened.

"What did this look like," he questioned, "seeing the glory of God?"

"It was like an 18 inch cylinder that came down from heaven," I replied.

I asked him if I could tell him of my encounter with Jesus.

"After hearing of your story so far, I'd love to hear more," he said.

So my testimony of my encounter with Jesus, my Bridegroom God followed.

"On January 20, 2010 I entered into this love encounter that followed a preparation of my heart days earlier," I explained. "It climaxed into a forty-five minute intense relationship encounter of love language that caused my heart to overflow."

He listened intently to all I had to say. "The Lord has done a great work in you," he said. "That excites me. I love to see God working!"

He listened to me express my love for God and God's love for me for nearly two hours. That was unusual as he normally had much to share about what he was continually learning.

He phoned me the next day. "I want you to know you released the Holy Spirit on me yesterday. Would you meet with a friend of mine? I would like you to share your experience with her."

"I'd be delighted," I replied, and we set a date for a few days later.

During that encounter I was not aware of a release. The Lord used him to make me more sensitive and aware of God's presence. I share this testimony to help believers be in tune with the Holy Spirit and know the release of His light when we speak forth the praises of His name. In this God is glorified. All praise, honor and glory be unto Him.

The Holy Spirit within Us

Our youngest son was attending elementary public school and doing well. He had made many friends and was making good grades. He seemed to be winning much favor with the teachers and was a content child.

I began receiving calls from one of his teachers. A problem was brewing. I finally responded to her, "the next time you phone I will come into the school."

Later, I realized from my son she took it to mean I would discipline him in class. At that point I knew praying for God's wisdom was the key. I could feel it was all about spiritual warfare. This young woman was not able to control her anger. She had no idea the enemy had a grip on her. I felt compassion for her as I know a classroom full of children would be a challenge.

It came to a head one day, when my husband and I returned from a trip out of the country. My son made me aware of the situation as soon as we returned, "Mother, you will be receiving a call from the teacher today," he explained, "she could not wait for your return."

I immediately phoned a prayer intercessor. "Do you have any suggestions as to what to do with this situation?"

"I suggest you call the school counselor and discuss it with him," she said. I took that advice.

I called the counselor, who replied, "I will set up a meeting with the teacher, principal and you to resolve this matter."

Delighted with his interest, I replied, "That would be great."

I prayed for the spirit of wisdom, and that the Holy Spirit would meet with us as I drove to the school. I walked into the meeting, and after introductions, the teacher was asked to give her story. She had a complaint he was a "bad boy," writing a "barn language" word on a sheet of paper on his desk in front of him. His fellow classmate had seen it and reported it to her. Then I was asked to speak. I wouldn't condone what my son had done, but I saw a spirit on her that was out of control and dealing badly with the matter. The Lord wanted me to help her with some direction.

The Holy Spirit was upon my first words. "What you have explained is exactly the story my son gave me," I began, "so I know he is telling the truth."

I felt a message of deep compassion welling up inside of me. I continued, "I understand the responsibility you carry as a teacher to speak "life" into the lives of each one of the children you have under your influence. This is a serious responsibility."

She began weeping uncontrollably. The principal left the room for a box of tissues. He returned, as I explained: "When you speak words that are negative such as 'bad boy' these are words that speak death into their spirit."

She looked at me with amazement. Her eyes told me this message was speaking to her, life was entering her spirit.

I went on. "The power of words and the power of the tongue, bring life or death, and we will eat its fruit. The words we speak to a person, especially a child, are words that direct their lives, words are that powerful. A child can go down a wrong path by hearing negative words. What they continually hear is what they are prone to follow. If we use positive words that speak life into our spirits, such as 'if you do this, you are a good boy,' the child will respond with joy and will delight in obedience from a positive word that brings the same message."

She continued to weep, convicted, and she pleaded with me. "What should I do next?"

"Apologize to the ones you are trying to influence, other teachers, and my son."

The teacher and the principle not only received what I said but thanked me for taking the time to come in and talk to them. I embraced her and blessed her; it was a time of encouragement for her heavy responsibility.

It was not me and my wisdom or influence that brought this matter to the open, but the magnificent mighty power of the Holy Spirit coming into the situation because of prayer. "The tongue has the power of life and death, and those who love it will eat its fruit" (Prov. 18:21). "Reckless words pierce like a sword, but the tongue of the wise brings healing" (Prov. 12:18). The Holy Spirit loves to be asked to come and help us. He is ready and willing.

I marvel at what God does when we pray.

Overcoming as We Walk in the Opposite Spirit

The next day my daughter approached me with a similar situation and asked, "Mother, would you please help me walk through a controlling attitude I am faced with today?" She had to go to a wholesaler to purchase some business items.

I could feel her despondence. "Yes, I'll spend the day with you, and find out what is happening."

On the way I explained our war is not against flesh and blood, but against principalities and powers. In order to overcome we must come in the opposite spirit. "A gentle answer turns away wrath, but a harsh word stirs up anger" (Prov. 15:1). In order to overcome a controlling spirit, we need to walk the love walk in our God given authority. Control is from the enemy and authority is from the Lord. She understood the principle, but was not sure how to walk it out.

As we walked in the front door, the woman at the front desk spoke harshly to my daughter as she asked her to show her pass. I walked to a table to set down the load I was carrying. I watched from a distance and prayed for the Lord to intervene. My daughter walked by me giving me the eye that it did not go well.

The woman followed her and approached me with both hands on her hips. Her lips curled and her eyes piercing she said, "I want you out that front door right now, your daughter's address on her ID is not the same as the address we have on record and you are not registered here, so gather up all your stuff and get out that door!"

I felt the Holy Spirit come as I began to speak, "So, my daughter's address does not match the address on your records, because her address is her home address and you have the business address. If I am not registered, I do have my identification with me and I can register."

Instantly her demeanor changed and she melted into a kind, soft woman. She became loving and courteous. With a smile she responded in a kind tone, "Well then, come to the front counter and I will add you to our files!" Filled with delight and joy in her step, she went to the front desk, and taking my identification filled out the forms with pleasant kindness. My daughter and I could hardly believe what happened.

When walking in the opposite spirit we take our God given authority and we are in charge as we walk in the Spirit of Christ. The Spirit within us is greater than the spirit in the world. We carry the power that is in Christ Jesus, the same power that raised Him from the dead. My daughter has always been a visual learner as many of us are. She was able to learn this concept by seeing it walked out. It made a lasting impression on both of us.

I hope this will encourage you in your walk with God. Walking with the Holy Spirit is power. God wants us to understand this in greater depth.

CHAPTER 8

Spiritual Authority

Brokenness is the only ground of true spiritual authority; complete surrender to the Lordship of Jesus Christ. The Kingdom belongs to the poor in spirit: "Blessed are the poor in spirit, for theirs is the kingdom of heaven" (Matt. 5:3). We need to be broken from our understanding of our selves. When we do, immediately supernatural identification with Jesus Christ takes place. Then the witness of God's Spirit is unmistakable: "I have been crucified with Christ and I no longer live, but Christ lives in me" (Gal. 2:20).

As we sign away our rights in complete surrender of obedience to our Master and Lord, we become Christ's ambassadors. "We are therefore Christ's ambassadors, as though God were making his appeal through us" (2 Cor. 5:20a).

What is an ambassador? He is a representative to a foreign country. So we are Christ's representatives on earth while Christ is in heaven. To understand the word ambassador better, let's look at the words the thesaurus gives us: authority, boss, captain, chief, commander, custodian, director, executive, judge, leader, manager, officer, overseer, premier, president, and supervisor. Perhaps this broadens our understanding. How do we represent Him? By walking in the authority He has given us. As we understand who we are in Christ, we have peace with God and with ourselves, and it brings peace with others.

Only when we know who we are and the authority we have through Him, can we be His ambassadors, walking in peace and confidence: "Be still and know that I am God" (Psalm 46:10). The Lord wants us to know who we are in Christ. I wasn't familiar with this idea, but the Lord revealed it to me in a remarkable way.

Revelation of "Who I Am in Christ"

I home schooled our children and took our son to his regular physical education session. Not knowing what to do for one hour, I pulled up to the shopping mall just to wait. A van began to pull out of a parking space so I could pull in. It stopped, and a woman I knew came from the passenger side and hurried to my window.

"There is a woman teaching in a church right now on 'who you are in Christ,'" she exclaimed with excitement. "It's for one hour, and it starts in three minutes. If you're interested, follow us."

"I'll follow you," I yelled out as she ran back to her van.

With that, they were down the street. I followed behind them feeling the amazing direction of God. Wasn't that His hand intervening in my life, guiding me as a loving Father does? As we walked in the class had just began, and we quietly found a place to sit. It was like a river began to flow; streams of living water. "To him who is thirsty I will give to drink without cost from the spring of the water of life" (Rev. 21:60). The thirst welled up and I drank, filled with truths I hadn't heard before. I wrote as fast as my little fingers could go.

The teacher spoke with rich enthusiasm. "We must overcome our insecurity, our fear, our guilt, our condemnation and our rejection." She began with those thought provoking words. "How are we to obtain that peace?" she added as she opened her Amplified Bible.

She began by reading Phil. 4:11: ". . . for I have learned how to be content (satisfied to the point where I am not disturbed or disquieted) in whatever state I am." She challenged us with the question, "How does this peace come about?"

The answer followed, "by being content, satisfied, not disturbed or disquieted." This surely was the answer to finding peace.

She continued stimulating our thoughts. "What is this source of this peace?" This left me eager to hear what the scriptures taught as she unfolded the Word of God. She took us to Romans 5:1. "Therefore, since we are justified (acquitted, declared righteous, and given a right standing with God) through faith, let us (grasp the fact that we) have (the peace of reconciliation) to hold and to enjoy, peace with God through our Lord Jesus Christ, the Messiah, the Anointed One."

"Our God is a God of peace and we are declared righteous and given a right with him," she said. "We must grasp the fact we have the peace of reconciliation and enjoy that peace with God procured by the shed blood of Jesus on the cross."

I began to see I could grasp onto this peace, not because I had anything to offer, but only through the finished work of Christ on the cross. He shed His blood so that I could live eternally with Him. He paid the debt, the price for my freedom. I have sinned but Christ has redeemed me. "Since all have sinned and are falling short of the honor and glory which God bestows and receives, (All) are justified and made upright and in right standing with God, freely and gratuitously by His grace (His unmerited favor and mercy), through the redemption which is (provided) in Christ Jesus" (Romans 3:23–24, Amplified Bible).

She further explained, "All have sinned, but all who believe have been justified. This is a truth we can grasp onto because it is the word of God."

I started to grasp these truths as the living water flowed into my spirit. I am a sinner, but I am free because of His shed blood, justified and made in right standing before God. It was like a light was shining into my understanding. My mind was transformed.

Peace: In Our Thoughts, Feelings, and Purposes

"Let our minds and our thoughts be transformed by the renewing of our minds" (Romans 12:2). I began to realize that my thinking was very important as she went on to explain Proverbs 23:7: "For as he thinks in his heart, so is he." I needed to get a hold of my thinking. I hadn't understood this before and these truths spoke to my spirit.

She proceeded to speak more truth. "Salvation has come to all men. The Gospel brings good news to men," she explained. "The word Gospel means "good news." The Lord wants us to walk in peace so we don't give the enemy any place in our lives."

Does this mean we open the door to the enemy if we do not walk in peace, I wondered?

She opened her Bible to John 14:27. "Peace I leave with you; My (own) peace I now give and bequeath to you. Not as the world gives do I give to you. Do not let your heart be troubled, neither let it be afraid." She added: "stop allowing yourselves to be agitated and disturbed; do not permit yourselves to be fearful, intimidated, cowardly, and unsettled" (AMP).

The words "do not permit yourself" stirred me. *Is this telling me I am responsible for my thoughts? If so, I cannot just allow my thinking to go uncontrolled.*

She explained another passage. "I have told you these things so that in Me you may have perfect peace and confidence. In the world you have tribulation and trials and distress and frustration; but be of good cheer—take courage, be confident, certain, undaunted—for I have overcome the world—I have deprived it of power to harm. I have conquered it (for you)" (John 16:33 AMP).

So I understood Jesus has conquered, has overcome, and we will also if we have His presence within us. And if we belong to Christ then we have the Holy Spirit within us.

She continued to bring us more of God's word, unfolding its truths step by step. As we know Christ we aren't bound by the power of sin. We are free, no longer a slave to sin, it no longer has a grip on us. "For sin shall not (any longer) exert dominion over you, since now you are not under law (as slaves), but under grace—as subjects of God's favor and mercy" (Romans 6:14 AMP).

As I read these Scriptures, the message of peace settled deep within my spirit. I felt the Holy Spirit unveiling my eyes, the Word of God becoming real to me. God wants us to be at peace with ourselves; in our thoughts, feelings, and purposes. I knew the Lord had sent His word and that it wouldn't return void. "So shall My word be that goes forth out of My mouth; it shall not return to Me void—without producing any effect, useless—but it shall accomplish that which I please and purpose, and it shall prosper in the thing for which I sent it" (Isaiah 55:11 AMP).

Secure in "Who We Are"

"Faith moves God," she added, "Fear moves the enemy. For God did not give us a spirit of timidity—of cowardice, of craven and cringing and fawning fear—but (He has given us a spirit) of power and of love and of calm and well-balanced mind and discipline and self-control" (2 Tim. 1:7 AMP).

"If we are secure in who we are," she continued, "we will see the effect of righteousness "And the effect of righteousness shall be peace (internal and external), and the result of righteousness, quietness and confident trust forever" (Is 32:17 AMP). "If we (freely) admit that we have sinned and confess our sins, He is faithful and just (true to His own nature and promises) and will forgive our sins (dismiss our lawlessness) and continuously cleanse us from all unrighteousness—everything not in conformity to His will in purpose, thought and action" (I John 1:9 AMP).

Ephesians 1:6 (AMP) tells us we are accepted in the beloved, "(So that we might be) to the praise and the commendation of His glorious grace—favor and mercy—which He so freely bestowed on us in the Beloved."

Our identity in Christ is not about our "do", it is about our "who." The "do" is all about the outward, and the "who" is all about the inward. Our heart is what matters to God. Moving in righteousness makes us acceptable to God : "(After all) the kingdom of God is not a matter of (getting the) food and drink (one likes), but instead, it is righteousness—that state which makes a person acceptable to God—and peace and joy in the Holy Spirit" (Romans 14:17 AMP).

We must be aware of the power of praise, and how it moves the hand of God. Praise is the highest expression of faith, see Psalm 149:6: "May the praise of God be in their mouths and a double-edged sword in their hands."

Winning the Battle

The biggest war we have is within ourselves, the battlefield of the mind. The true knowledge of God fills us with peace. 2 Peter 1:2 (AMP) teaches us: "May grace (God's favor) and peace, (which is perfect well-being, all necessary good, all spiritual prosperity, freedom from fears and agitating passions and moral conflicts) be multiplied to you in (the full, personal, precise and correct) knowledge of God and of Jesus our Lord."

As I received the word of God and soaked in the truth that the lady spoke, it transformed me. My mind was renewed by the Word accompanied by His Spirit. The closing verse, Philippians 4:4, moved me: "Rejoice in the Lord always—delight, gladden yourselves in Him; again I say, Rejoice!"

The concept of authority was not easy to understand. But the Lord gave me this clear message of who I am in Christ: "I will give you the keys of the kingdom of heaven; whatever you bind on earth will be bound in heaven, and whatever you loose on earth will be loosed in heaven" (Matt. 16:19 NIV). I was so startled with this message I couldn't tell anyone for several days. Then, unable to hold it in, I eventually had to share it. I had the faith to believe it, but it was overwhelming. To have the keys to the kingdom of heaven? That much authority was hard to understand; it was sobering. But my prayers needed to be from a surrendered heart; no agenda of my own, but a heart in love with God.

Paul instructed in Titus 2:15 (AMP) "Tell (them all) these things. Urge (advise, encourage, warn) and rebuke with full authority. Let no one despise or disregard or think little of you—conduct yourself and your teaching so as to command respect." These encourage us to teach with authority. We encourage and rebuke as both are necessary in the body of Christ.

A further idea of authority followed: to trample on snakes and scorpions! "Behold! I have given you authority and power to trample upon serpents and scorpions, and (physical and mental strength and ability) over all the power that the enemy (possesses), and nothing shall in any way harm you" (Luke 10: 19 AMP).

Praying in Tongues

The Lord then brought me into a new level of authority in prayer. "Janet, you need to be speaking in tongues!" These words were spoken over me as I sensed the presence of the Holy Spirit. But an intense battle went on inside me. My spirit was drawn but my mind fought what I heard; the spirit warring against the flesh. I was compelled by the spirit but my mind was saying, *No, this is not right, tongues have ceased with the apostles, and maybe it was even of the devil.*

However, I recalled a month earlier all four of our children received it in one day. It began early in the morning with our oldest son. He laid hands on several others and they were baptized in the Holy Spirit, all receiving tongues at once. By the end of the day, thirteen youth had been baptized in the Spirit and all spoke in tongues. Many felt a deep deliverance as this happened. They saw visions of enemy forces leaving, received deliverance from bondages; one saw a snake leave and a dragon. The Holy Spirit worked with such intense power some of them began to shake. I was still trying to understand the move of the Holy Spirit that day and the days following. Now I was torn, confronted with this new message.

As I allowed the Holy Spirit to be my teacher, I listened to what this man had to bring to me from the Lord. He said, "You must speak in tongues and I have a book you need to read that I will give you, the name of it is *Praying with Fire*, by Barbara Billett." I felt the compelling of the Holy Spirit that I must listen and be obedient. I was beginning to be sensitive to the Holy Spirit and I did not want to grieve Him, so He would leave me. I could not live without communion with the Holy Spirit.

Within a couple of days, I received this book and I was excited to read it. I read, "If you want tongues, all you need to say is, 'Lord, if tongues is of you, and if you want me to have tongues, I believe.'" I could hardly believe what I read. My mind fought against those words; I thought they were ridiculous. But I jumped up from the chair, went out the door, and down the road for a prayer walk. After nearly 30 minutes time with the Lord, while returning home, I recalled those words: "If you want tongues, all you need to say is, 'Lord, if tongues is of you, and if you want me to have tongues, I believe.'"

I pondered that statement for a moment. That would be safe to pray because I was releasing myself into the hands and presence of God. "Have me Lord. Not my will but Yours will be done." I thought, *I can add, "Lord, if tongues is of you"*; it was added assurance. I was safe with that prayer. Again, I added: "If you want me to have tongues." Yes, even if tongues is of the Lord, it may not be for me. I was aware it could cause great turmoil in my life, as family and friends would reject me. So it may not be for me. But, I released it to the Lord.

I spoke those words. I remember saying, "I believe" although my belief was no larger than a grain of mustard seed. But that's all it took for the power of God to come upon me. My mouth opened and I began to speak this foreign language with intense speed. My little tongue had never experienced anything so rapid.

Here I was out in the middle of the open country, just God and I, speaking in tongues rapidly and there was no way I could stop. I continued to walk up to our home but felt I could not go back until I was able to stop, so I proceeded beyond our home. I needed to figure out how to stop this speech from continuing. Still concerned, I decided to return home; there seemed no alternative. As I approached, our daughter drove in. Immediately I thought, *I know I can approach her and hug her with a Hello and begin speaking to her.* But I had no control over my speech. I began to speak even more rapidly.

My mind was completely free, separate from my spirit. My spirit was praying to God while my mind sought to understand what was happening. I wondered what it would take to stop, I was becoming very tired, but my mind made no impact. Perhaps if I made a call to my husband I would surely be able to speak to him, I went into the house and made the call.

The phone rang. "Good afternoon, this is Peter." I heard his voice.

He listened as I spoke in tongues rapidly. "Hello?" another wait. Silence on his end.

I tried to speak to him, but had no control of my speech. He listened. He called my cell phone on another line. My daughter answered.

"What is happening," he asked in a concerned voice.

"Mommy is speaking in tongues and cannot stop."

I began to groan as a woman in travail. I felt like I was giving birth as I had with my children. My husband put down his phone, and rushed home, wondering what could be happening. I felt desperate. I didn't know what to do next. I was exhausted, completely overwhelmed. I put my head down between my knees groaning, took my hands and cupped them over my mouth using all my strength and finally stopped speaking. I sat there for a moment feeling like I had just given birth, when my husband walked in.

"So you were just speaking in tongues, do it again," he said. He wanted to see and hear what this was all about,

I responded, "You don't approach a woman that has just had a baby and say 'have another baby!'"

I felt as worn out as I did following the deliveries of our four children. It took me three days of laying low to get my strength back.

For several days I walked in fear that it would happen again. What would I do? But I soon came to understand speaking in tongues is voluntary. I can speak it like a person that decides to speak another language. It is a language, a heavenly language, and I felt blessed.

Revelation of Tongues

The Lord began to show me the power of tongues. A couple of weeks later Peter asked if I speak in tongues every day.

I responded, "No, I don't understand tongues. Every time someone interprets my speech they say it's 'Praise the Lord, Hallelujah.' I know the Lord inhabits the praises of His people but saying 'Hallelujah, Praise the Lord' for an hour doesn't make sense to me, I need to figure this stuff out."

So the next day I decided to close myself behind the french doors of our living room. I prayed, "Lord, I will sit here and pray in tongues for one hour. I need to figure out what tongues is all about." I looked at my watch and set the time and started. After a couple of minutes I thought it may be helpful for my eight year old son to help me figure it out. Still speaking intensely I found him, motioned for him to follow me to the living room. I began to write messages to him on paper. I asked him to pray for the spirit of interpretation. He went across the room, and kneeled to pray. Shortly after, he sat on the couch beside me. "Mother," he said, "I just heard you say 'Hallelujah, Praise the Lord' three times." I thought I heard the same thing and he confirmed it.

Then I heard myself say "Lord help him . . ." I wrote this message to my son, then added "let's ask the Lord—help him do what?" Then I wondered, *help who?* So in my understanding I prayed, "Lord, I pray for Peter." As I said "Peter" I heard myself say "Peter" in the foreign tongue, with a strong roll on the "r": "Ptrrr." I kept hearing Peter's name; I knew I was praying for my husband.

Excitement welled up inside me. I thought of Amanda on a trip; she needed protection. I simply said: "Lord, I pray for Amanda." As I said Amanda in my understanding I could clearly hear Amanda, again with a strong roll on the "r": "mrrrnda." I kept hearing her name. *I must be learning something,* I thought. *Our son Jason possibly needs prayer too.* So again, I prayed in my understanding: "Lord, I pray for Jason." Immediately I heard "Jason," with a rolling "dr": "drrrason."

Amazement hit me. I stopped praying and thought, *No one has ever told me what speaking in tongues is all about. This is truly amazing.*

Days later my husband, daughter and I were praying for the ministry my husband was leading. We prayed through a long list and I concluded: "let me pray in the spirit for each one and let's circle the name when we hear it." We completed the list. Then Peter asked me to continue, as he had received many written out prayer requests on email. I took a pen to use as a pointer on the screen as I was speaking the words in a foreign tongue. Each request was tracked, the words were obvious in a foreign language. We could hardly believe what we heard. I had no more doubt that tongues was from the Lord and the gift of tongues was for me.

Prayer and Prophecy

Soon after that, through interpretation of what I said, I realized that at times I was praying and other times I was receiving revelation through prophecy. I realized there is a praying in tongues and there is a speaking in tongues to receive revelation.

One month before all four of our children received the gift of tongues, I realized something was happening in our circle of influence, as I tried to understand what was happening in my own life. Our journey was beginning. The word of God began to open to us. First, 1 Corinthians 14 came alive and rich for the first time in my life; its mysteries unfolded, beginning with 1 Cor. 14:2–5:

> For anyone who speaks in a tongue does not speak to men but to God. Indeed, no one understands him; he utters mysteries with his spirit . . . He who speaks in a tongue edifies himself . . . I would like everyone of you to speak in tongues . . .

As these words gave meaning to my understanding, they became rich. I was speaking to God. No one understood me–I did not even understand myself. I did understand I was uttering mysteries with my spirit and receiving revelation from God. In addition, when my spirit felt weak it would edify and strengthen me. The Lord wanted me to speak in tongues.

For if I pray in a tongue, my spirit prays, but my mind is
unfruitful. So what shall I do? I will pray with my spirit, but
I will also pray with my mind; I will sing with my spirit, but
I will also sing with my mind. 1 Cor. 14:14–15

The Lord gave clear revelation of these Scriptures. I was praying
with my mind, but I could also hear those prayers in the spirit. When I
prayed for a person I could hear the name in another language. Clearly
my spirit prayed when my mind was unfruitful. Speaking in tongues
with my son, I wrote him seven pages of notes as we tried to understand
what God would reveal to us. It was only later reading 1 Corinthians
14, that everything I had just learned was spelled out perfectly. Then I
knew it was from God.

Verse 26 states: "What then shall we say, brothers? When you
come together, everyone has a hymn, or a word of instruction, a
revelation, a tongue or an interpretation. All of these must be done for
the strengthening of the church." Realizing it strengthened my spirit,
I saw it strengthening for the body of Christ also. Speaking in tongues
is powerful in the body for direction and those things that need prayer.

Learning Powerful Prayer

Peter and I were on a cruise with a ministry team, when Peter felt
overwhelmed with the responsibility as the prayer leader, and connecting
properly with each ministry head. He could not see his way through it.
He had ten to twelve couples to minister to, and not feeling unity in
the team discouraged him.

The gift of tongues was still new to me. Not knowing the full effect
of this gift, I suggested I would pray in tongues for twenty or thirty
minutes before each meeting. By the time we left the ship we had
learned the heightened effects that tongues brought into our lives. The
presence of God was evident at each meeting, the bonding and unity
was so strong. We knew God had gone before us and heard my prayers
although I did not understand them. The spirit made intercession when
my mind was unfruitful.

We sat in what my husband thought would be the most difficult meeting. But we heard, "Peter, our president has changed much in this organization, but the best change has been bringing you on board!" We heard another response., "Peter, you have been the means of bringing the Holy Spirit into this organization." The favor granted amazed us. It was evident God went before us.

A few years later, we went through a most difficult time financially. We were desperate, not knowing where to turn next. Peter wondered how he would make it through that week. I reminded my husband of the time God responded on the cruise, and we saw God's miracle. I felt compelled to pray steadily until I saw a breakthrough. A day or two later, my husband made a phone call to a previous contact and landed a large project that put us back on our feet. Twice during negotiating, it seemed to be falling through, but as I prayed in the spirit it came together in a miraculous way. Every time it seemed the deal would go sideways, I prayed in the spirit until the deal was signed.

"Open Our Hearts, Lord". . . . God Wants to Move

We searched the Scriptures for the truth of His Word, and read in Acts 17:11:"Now the Bereans were of more noble character than the Thessalonians, for they received the message with great eagerness and examined the Scriptures every day to see if what Paul said was true." The answers are in the Word of God. We are called to examine the Scriptures every day to verify what others say.

I have found speaking in tongues reveals hidden mysteries, brings edification and strength into my spirit. Speaking in tongues is also a hidden key to moving in the power and anointing of the Holy Spirit. It is no wonder that the devil has fought against speaking in tongues. Those who are hungry and thirsty for the Lord can trust the promise of Jesus. It is real for today because "Jesus Christ is the same yesterday, today, and forever" (Heb. 13: 8).

Missionaries in Africa have the privilege of seeing crowds of more than 50,000 at once receive the baptism of the Holy Spirit with speaking in tongues during mass evangelism campaigns. These stories are exciting and must be amazing to see.

Those who speak in tongues will often operate in other gifts as well. For example, they will lay hands on and pray for the sick according to Mark 16:15–18. Those who do not regularly speak in tongues will also not normally move in other gifts. In fact, they will frequently oppose participation in other gifts. Baptism in the Holy Spirit with speaking in tongues certainly seems to be the entrance to moving in other gifts. This is probably why the enemy of revival, Satan, will fight so hard to discredit those who move in tongues and other gifts. If Satan cannot discourage people from receiving the baptism of the Holy Spirit with tongues, he will try to bring discredit to the movement of the Spirit by denying the truths of Scripture and fomenting tension between believers. Some with extreme views suggest all believers will speak in tongues. But tongues may not necessarily be a gift for every believer. I know it was a gift the Lord wanted for me, and I encourage each believer to ask the Lord if it is a gift He wants to release to them.

A close friend of mine has prayed for tongues much of her life wanting it earnestly, but has never received it. She loves the Lord but has never received that gift. God is sovereign and He reigns.

Dreams of Revelation

Soon after I received the gift of tongues I was confronted with: "Janet, have you prayed for dreams?" I wasn't sure this was relevant for today. But constantly questioned by a very good friend, I realized she would stop only if I said "yes" instead of "no." The pressure was causing me to become weary, so, in my quiet time I prayed a simple prayer, thinking it really would make no effect because I had no understanding for dreams. I just prayed, 'Lord, please give me dreams.' That was the extent of the prayer, short and simple. It felt good. I could honestly tell my friend, I had prayed for dreams, and released the pressure. I had doubt of the reality of this gift of God.

Only a couple of days later, my husband and I were on a trip for several days. While in a motel I had a dream. This dream was unusual. I had normal dreams before, but I knew there was something very different about this one. I continued to question the reality of this new concept and did not want to say anything to my husband. Later on that day we wound up in a restaurant with a gift shop and I was drawn to a book. Returning to our motel I could not wait to read the book I had bought. The author explained a dream he had, and I found myself saying to my husband, "I had a dream last night." We both knew it was a spiritual dream.

In the dream I was driving a car with another woman in the passenger seat. I was driving fast, weaving around all the cars in my way. My speed was steady but faster than any other car on the road. The freeway was eight lanes wide and I was able to find an opening to pass as I was unable to brake and slow down. Suddenly, all eight lanes were full so I crossed to the shoulder of the road. It was narrow but paved. I went over the white line, rushing around the end vehicle when I noticed a plastic container in front of me. It was about two feet wide and three feet long, open with no lid and laying on its side. I saw there was nothing inside it but I freaked out. I woke up as I hit it.

As I explained this dream to my husband, he said, "That is very simple. The vehicle is ministry and you are going so fast you think you are out of control and things in your life will scare you. But it is no big deal. A plastic container will not do any damage as you run over it. You need not fear."

Teaching of God's Word

The dreams began that night and have continued at an increasing rate. Some nights the Lord will give me three dreams: of instruction, warning, revelation, or encouragement; whatever the Lord wants to say to me. Sometimes it is a message to give instruction to another person. The word of God opened up to me in a new dimension as the Lord began giving me dreams. I saw how God is the same yesterday, today, and forever.

What does the Word have to teach us about dreams?

In Genesis 41:1, Pharaoh had a dream and in verses 15 and 16: "Pharaoh said to Joseph, 'I had a dream, and no one can interpret it. But I have heard it said of you that when you hear a dream you can interpret it.' 'I cannot do it,' Joseph replied to Pharaoh, 'but God will give Pharaoh the answer he desires.'" We see this dream was a revelation from the Lord.

Again, in Daniel 2:1 Nebuchadnezzar had dreams. His mind was troubled and he could not sleep, and he inquired as to their meaning. In verse 19: "During the night the mystery was revealed to Daniel in a vision." Daniel had a dream of four beasts in Daniel 7. Job speaks of being frightened with dreams in Job 7:14. Gideon had a dream and its interpretation and worshiped God. He called out, "Get up! The Lord has given the Midianite camp into your hands," in Judges 7:15. The Lord appeared to Solomon in a dream during the night in 1 Kings 3:5.

An angel of the Lord appeared to Joseph in a dream in Matthew 1:20. ". . . do not be afraid to take Mary home as your wife, because what is conceived in her is from the Holy Spirit." And again in chapter 2:12. "And having been warned in a dream not to go back to Herod, they returned to their country by another route." We see the same again in verses 13, 19, and 22. We read in Joel 2:28 and in Acts 2:17 that in the Day of the Lord, the global harvest ". . . your old men will dream dreams, your young men will see visions."

This is what the Lord has for His people among the many other things before the coming of the great and the dreadful Day of the Lord. The Lord wants to give instruction by His Spirit. We need to be open to what the Lord has for us, and the way He desires to reveal it to us. This took me out of my "box," bringing me to a completely new way of revelation according to His Word. The Holy Spirit leads us into "all truth." As we surrender our own agenda to Him, the Word of God teaches us He will lead and guide us. That is a precious place to be.

The Watchman Calling

The Lord brought me to a new concept as I understood new levels of spiritual authority. He impressed upon my heart the revelation of a watchman. The book, *The Harbinger,* by Jonathan Cahn, addresses the signs of the past repeated in the present and shows only repentance can break the judgment that will happen again. It is a novel about a man named Nouriel having unexpected encounters with an unknown prophet who speaks truth about the nation, and that only repentance will change the tide. The last words in this book were accompanied with the overwhelming power of the Holy Spirit; it hit me as I read the final charge the prophet gave to Nouriel:

> So, then, take up your trumpet, Nouriel,
> Set it to your mouth and blow,
> Let the sound of the watchmen be heard in the city,
> Let the call of redemption cover the land,
> Let the word go forth and have its way,
> And let those who have ears to hear it . . .
> Let them hear it,
> And be saved.

The Lord is calling forth watchmen. Responsibility comes with what has been entrusted to us. We don't want to be guilty that our city sleeps and the people are ignorant. We are entrusted with their awakening and redemption. We may not feel adequate or ready. Do you think Moses felt ready? Or Jeremiah, or Mary, or Peter? We need to remember it's not about us. It's all about Him!

What God told Ezekiel to do in the Old Testament, Jesus tells us to do now. God told Ezekiel to speak to all the lost and perishing in the house of Israel. Similarly, Jesus tells us to speak to all the lost and perishing around us. In His final words before returning to heaven, Jesus gave us the great commission.

Therefore go and make disciples of all nations, baptizing them in the name of the Father and of the Son and of the Holy Spirit, and teaching them to obey everything I have commanded you. And surely I am with you always, to the very end of the age. (Matt. 28: 19-20)

CHAPTER 9

Authority through Unity in Marriage

... then make my joy complete by being likeminded, having
the same love, being one in spirit and purpose. (Phil. 2:2)

Unity is a threat to the enemy.

My husband and I thought we had a very good marriage. Then the
Lord revealed it could use some improvement.

So what did that mean? The Lord was showing us that to have
authority against the forces of the enemy our marriage needed to achieve
a higher level. He gently and graciously taught us that we cannot go into
spiritual warfare without the proper authority.

As we walk together in unity as a couple and with the Lord, we
gain authority. The Lord revealed ways that would bring us to a deeper
connection with each other. The importance of this concept provoked
us to search for answers. We implemented ideas the Lord gave us into
our God given temperaments.

When God molds us we complement one another, as a hand in a
glove fit together. Where I am weak my husband is strong and where my
husband is weak I am strong. The Lord gave us direction to build into
each other as we opened ourselves to the Lord's revelation. I encourage
each couple to do the same.

Many times we have sins or handicaps we are not aware of that hinder our walk with the Lord. Who sees it better than our partner? They know us more intimately than any one; they can help us see and overcome better than we can.

My greatest hindrance was the spirit of rejection, but my husband helped me walk through the revelation. It seemed like a battle I would never win. One day I said, "I don't think I will ever get rid of this rejection spirit." I really thought it impossible.

I did not have faith to believe it was possible and it seemed like I was cursing myself. At that moment I repented for opening the door to that spirit, and asked the Lord for forgiveness. I maintained that repentant spirit and was able to become completely free as I walked through this hindrance with my husband. He encouraged and helped me as the Lord gave him direction for our marriage. That's what it took for us to reach a new level in our marriage.

How I Met My Husband

The Lord brought my husband to me in a remarkable way; it was His guiding and directing hand. I had dated several guys and wondered if the right one would ever come along. My sisters said many times, "when you meet the right one you will know it." It seemed I never knew it. But one day my brother called me as I finished work.

"What're you doing for the weekend?" he asked.

"Going to visit our sister. I'm packing and hope to be gone in an hour or so."

"No, I have a fella I want you to meet," he said. "Just happen to be at my house at 2:00 tomorrow afternoon and you will meet him."

I was speechless. It was out of character for my brother to recommend a man to me. So I pondered the idea.

"Yes, okay, I'll try to make that work."

My brother went on: "I met him a couple of weeks ago when he came to my shop for the sale of a truck. We talked and I've spent some time with him since. I want you to meet him."

My curiosity was strong enough to change my plans and follow his suggestion. I went to his house with my mother, but no one showed. The house was under construction so I knew the timing was planned precisely, so after 20 minutes we returned to my parents' home. Thirty minutes later the door bell rang. My father responded to the ring; he opened the door to my brother.

"Dad, I want to introduce you to Peter. He has a business and he may need some brochures printed."

My brother made up the excuse to bring him over so we could meet. We listened to the conversation for a minute from another room. Then my mother suggested, "let's go meet them." She took the lead and introduced herself. I followed.

"Hello, glad to meet you," I said. He returned the greeting, and I sat down.

I immediately felt an attraction and wanted to get to know this man. I thought, *his conversation was directed towards my father but he's snatching a look at me from time to time.* My father, a very sociable man, led the conversation but told me later he clearly did not have Peter's attention. My father and I waved them good-bye and returned to the living room.

Out of the blue, I blurted out, "someday he is going to be my husband."

I was astonished at what I said. The words came out of my mouth without thought. This puzzled me. I heard my voice speaking but my mind was not engaged. My heart was saying, *I want to get to know this man.* How did that happen? I asked myself this question for 20 years. Then one day as I was giving this testimony I realized I was speaking in the prophetic. Prophetic words are given by people as they speak from their spirit.

Peter left our town knowing there was an unusual connection with me. It seemed he had met the girl who was to be his wife. It was strong enough to scare him. The power and presence of God upon him woke him up in the night. That same intense power did not come upon him again for 20 years. When it returned to him, he knew it was the power of God that hit him the day we met.

Be Like Minded

Our marriage has always been very dear to our hearts. My focus has always been my husband and my children, that they would be happy and walking with the Lord. Employed in the working world before I married, I knew the challenges and the confidence that working with people can give. I was office manager of a large insurance company and secretary for an orthodontist/dentist, and a legal secretary before I married. I left this all behind when I married; I wanted to raise a family and be the woman in the home.

When our children reached their teen years we sensed the call to a higher level of intimacy with God and with each other. As this burned in our hearts, the Lord brought us into the Word: "Husbands, in the same way be considerate as you live with your wives, and treat them with respect as the weaker partner and as heirs with you of the gracious gift of life, so that nothing will hinder your prayers" (1 Peter 3: 7). It was essential to love God and each other unconditionally.

God was looking for a husband-and-wife team to run the race together. We knew we would not be ministering together all the time, but God wanted us to support each other even when we were ministering apart. The key is, "Be like-minded, having the same love, being one in spirit and purpose." This is where unity is born, the foundation for the authority we need.

One time, when Peter was in Panama, he was asked to speak to 65 denominational leaders. He felt he had a message from the Lord but was unsure what it was when he left. But the day before he spoke he sensed it was "unity in marriage." This message gripped the hearts of the people. That this was a message the Lord had for these people was confirmed later. Later, Peter heard many pastors preached this message. The Lord often speaks the same message to His people in different places. This was confirmation that God used the message in a powerful way across the country.

I was given a book, *Marketplace, Marriage and Revival*, by Jack Serra which covered what the Lord was teaching us. He writes:

Reaching the marketplace for Christ requires tremendous prayer. Being a godly worker in the marketplace requires a tremendous marriage. But what if your prayers are being hindered because of your marriage?

First Peter 3: 7 tells us that we're to treat our wives a certain way so that nothing will hinder our prayers. The word hinder means "to cause delay, retard or hamper." It also means "to prevent from happening." Wouldn't it be a shame to be praying daily for your business and the marketplace, only to have your prayers be hindered by the quality of your marriage? It can happen. Have you ever wondered why your prayers aren't being answered? Could it be because of the way you consider and treat your wife?'

How exciting is it to know and understand the ways of the Lord, the truths of God's word speaking to our spirit and then to cry out for God's grace to empower us to walk it out! Our focus can be easily distracted with the busyness of life and we are not aware a marriage that may be deteriorating. This is not the plan of God for our lives. Our prayers are hindered and our ministry is dwarfed.

Reaching the marketplace for Christ is dependent on our marriage. Isn't this sobering? This needs to get our attention: our city will be won from our bedrooms! Has this ever occurred to you? I didn't understand this until the Lord began to lead us into this truth—a truth the Lord wants me to share with you so we can walk it out together.

So an important key to reaching our city through the marketplace is our marriage. We cannot expect to fulfill the instruction in Philippians 2:1–5 corporately if we are not fulfilling them in the first and most important relationship, our marriage. Paul exhorts us to be like-minded, having the same love and being one in spirit and purpose . . . to do nothing out of selfish ambition or vain conceit, but in humility, to consider others better than ourselves. We are also commanded to look to the interests of others. These verses apply directly to our marriages, and if we are double-minded about how necessary a sound marriage is, we cannot reach the marketplace for Christ, let alone our city.

Being Obedient to His Voice

During this time, we woke one morning with a surprise. The Lord was stirring my husband's heart to take me on an outing out of character for him: to spend a day together buying me several new outfits. I did not feel it necessary, but it was a day filled with fun. A bonding took place. Small things are important. The Lord wants us to honor one another, and that day honor was the focus. As he honored me, I honored him for the grace he exhibited. It brought a new depth of understanding for each other. It was not an ordinary day of shopping; we felt the Lord speaking to our spirits.

Several months later we joined a group from Canada to tour Argentina and met many of the men and women that took part in a revival there.

We landed in Buenos Aires. My husband handed our passports to the customs officer. She looked at them and then directly at Peter.

"Mr. Van Hierden, your passport has expired!"

Peter's heart sank to his shoes. He looked at me in shock.

She continued, "we cannot allow you in our country, you must be confined and return on the first available flight."

I wondered what would happen to us now. We were there with two children and I could not imagine spending two weeks apart from my husband after planning family time together.

"How did this happen," my husband whispered to me. "No one caught this until I landed at my destination. It was not detected by three authorities: first the Canadian customs, then, by two airlines which is an automatic fine of five thousand dollars to each airline."

God must have blinded their eyes, because He wanted Peter in Buenos Aires, but the Lord also used this occasion to highlight once again: He wanted us to excel in unity in our marriage.

"Come with me," the officer ordered. "Wait in this room until we can send you back on the next returning flight."

We parted, and I met the waiting party with my children. As a group we were scheduled to meet with several prophetic teams that were part of the revival that began in Argentina in 1985. My husband was locked alone in a small room with a chair, table and a computer. He had many hours to think, pray and spend time with God. He opened his emails. The first was from a ministry and this is what he read:

> Daddy's Girls. (Girls that belong to God) Well, this is an encouragement word although it doesn't sound like it at first. But it's for the guys, i.e. husbands, brothers, fathers, sons. God has let some things come to the surface today. Your daughters, mothers, wives, sisters, and aunts are DADDY'S GIRLS. You are going to have to treat them right—not only right, but special. Treat them like a queen, honor them, and God will honor you. Sorry, but some of you are going to the woodshed for a spanking from Dad. So maybe do some repenting and changing—it is time.
>
> . . . So there it is. Treat your wives, sisters, daughters, mothers, grandmothers, and aunts, etc. like princesses because they are GOD'S PRINCESSES. You are a prince— why not behave like one?

Immediately the Lord reminded him of his agitated spirit towards me earlier that day. He saw he could not get by with what he thought earlier was nothing. Later, when he was able to contact me and apologize I could not recall the occasion. Nothing had affected me as I remembered nothing.

He explained, "I said some cross words, because I recall being agitated in my spirit, although I don't remember what it was about."

"I surely accept your apology, honey," I responded somewhat puzzled.

We sat in amazement. We must listen when the Lord wants our attention, and He often seeks our attention when we least expect it. The moment he repented before the Lord and to me a release took place in Peter's spirit, and God was so pleased. We both wept feeling how much God loves us and wants us to walk in obedience. God is so loving.

Answered Prayer

The team and I began to pray for Peter. Also a group of local prayer warriors began to pray. One of them had a connection with an official at the Canadian Embassy, who began to work on Peter's behalf. After eight hours using all her connections and persuasive skills, she was able to furnish Peter with a temporary visa while the passport was being issued. The visa was approved by the Argentinian officials, on the condition a renewed passport would be issued later that week before he left the country.

He was released after twelve hours in confinement, just thirty minutes before he was scheduled to board the plane to return home.

This was a miracle. The Canadian Embassy official issued a Canadian passport to my husband. As she handed it to him, she said, "you are a very lucky man, because this is the last Canadian passport that will be issued from this office. A ruling came down that we can no longer issue passports." Yes, we had favor with many people working together to make this happen; their hearts were in the hands of the Lord.

I share this testimony to demonstrate the unity the Lord desires from us as a couple. Unity in our marriages brings authority as we pray. This is what the Lord wants for you. Ask the Lord for more of His grace, He is waiting for you. The Lord began to drop impressions in our hearts: to spend more time together talking, dating, walking; even cooking together.

Being Sensitive to the Holy Spirit

Becoming more sensitive to the Holy Spirit, I became aware of the strategy of the enemy to quench the Holy Spirit. I wept inside if my relationship with my husband grieved the Holy Spirit. We knew we had come to a new level of unity in our marriage. We discussed how we would communicate that sensitivity. We wanted to be sufficiently aware we could nip it in the bud if either of us felt the quenching of the Spirit. We both felt safe being on guard for each other, and sharing that depth of unity.

The next morning it was tested.

It is Sunday morning. I'm doing my hair in the bathroom at the head of the stairs. My daughter is beside me and we are chatting and laughing together. I'm not paying attention to the time. I hear my husband's footsteps coming up the stairs. I know I'm in trouble as he doesn't like to be late for church.

I cringe! This is going to quench the Holy Spirit if it's handled badly. I should have watched the time. It's important to work through this; if we quench the Holy Spirit and enter the house of the Lord with an edge in our spirit, we will not feel His presence. I know the enemy is waiting for an open door. I need to respond appropriately.

"Honey, we need to leave, or we will be late for church," he announces.

I thought it best not to respond with words. I give him the agreed expression; he understands and immediately returns downstairs.

I apologized on the way to church. During the worship I felt the love of God flowing. The Holy Spirit met with us and I basked in His presence. The Holy Spirit wants us to be responsible for His presence. He is gentle in nature and waits to be invited and welcomed into our lives. So we became very intentional to sense His presence because we did not want Him to leave. This needs to become part of our nature. We need this grace each day.

An incident confirmed this to me one day in Cape Town, South Africa. While attending a conference there, my husband was visiting with the speaker and I quietly pulled up a chair to join them. He looked at me and said, "you are an intercessor, you have a lot of authority." He had never met me before and knew nothing about me. The Lord used him to confirm the journey the Lord was taking us on.

I hope this testimony encourages you to unify your marriage so your prayers are not hindered; that we may all come in prayer to God with authority and He will hear us.

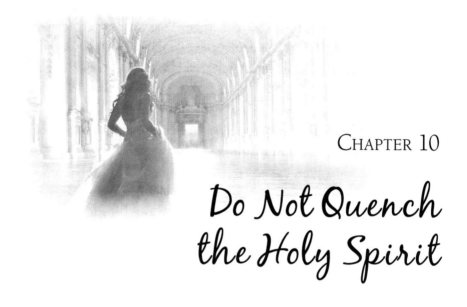

Do Not Quench the Holy Spirit

"Do not put out the Spirit's fire . . . Do not quench (suppress or subdue) the (Holy) Spirit." (1 Thess. 5:19. Amplified Bible)

We are the children of God and the Holy Spirit lives within. "He lives with you and will be in you" (John 14: 17b). Through the power of the Holy Spirit the believer can acquire revelation of the Word of God, be led by the Spirit, experience His continual presence, understand the plans of God, and become a bold witness for Christ.

The Holy Spirit is very sensitive and can be quenched if we do not cultivate communion with Him. We can grieve Him without being aware of it.

Learning a Lesson the Hard Way

Sitting in a movie theatre together with my husband one evening, I felt incredible pain. My left ankle hurt as I set my foot down in the parking lot. It felt like something gave as it touched the ground.

I tried to ignore it as I walked inside, but as the pain continued to increase. I went into the washroom and rubbed it to ease the pain. Nothing helped. I felt embarrassed thinking I may have to tell the

111

couple that invited us I would have to leave. It was my friend's birthday, and they had invited us to the movie, "The Titanic." Within minutes, scenes in this movie made it evident that it was not a place for us to be spending the evening.

My husband and I hadn't been to a theatre together before. I felt honored that my friend chose us to celebrate her special day; it was hard to say no to her. So I convinced my husband we should go, as she was a close friend and I didn't want to disappoint her.

The pain continued to increase and I thought elevating my foot would help. I hung my foot over my husband's knee. It did not help.

"My foot is in terrible pain," I whispered to my husband. "We need to go."

He turned to me with a questioning look. "What's happening," he asked.

"I don't know, but the pain is awful, let's go."

"Okay, we can go if you like, but let's tell our friends we need to leave."

"Yes, but I can't walk, you will need to carry me out."

My husband took me up in his arms and carried me to the car. An embarrassing moment. I checked in to the hospital emergency as my foot turned black. The doctors tested me for everything they considered might be the cause. The pain eased through the night and I was released in the morning. I've had no problems with the foot after that evening.

It remains a mystery in the physical, but not in the spiritual. The Lord drew us out of a place that was quenching the presence of God in our lives. The enemy wants to quench the Holy Spirit so we cannot discern truth from error. I was pulled in by the influence of a friend. That entertainment might be alright for them, but not for us. Each person needs to know for themselves.

The Lord has a gracious way of leading his children in the way they should go. Quenching the Holy Spirit is quenching the life within us. We need to be mindful of the places we go, what we do, the people we associate with. This all affects the life within us. The Lord put his finger on me, not my husband, as I was the one that led us into that place. It was a trap of the enemy, but the Lord was gracious and gently removed us in a loving way.

I hope this testimony speaks to you as it did to me as I walked through it. May you learn from my mistakes. As the saying goes, a wise man learns from his mistakes, but an even wiser man learns from another's mistakes.

Under Proper Cover

The Lord continued to lay it heavily on my heart not to quench the Holy Spirit. This time it was through a dream that woke me at 2:00 a.m. It was a serious warning of spiritual death to me if I did not heed it, and it could not wait till morning. We were at a resort in the mountains in meetings with a ministry strategy group for a couple of days. Surely I could get interpretation with so many pray-ers.

In my dream, I was on my hands and knees in a large garden, cultivating with a small rake and shovel, and turning the soil to plant seeds. The soil was dark and rich. But it was full of poisonous worms that killed anyone they bit; a dangerous place to be working. Anyone working this garden needed a cover person watching over them to immediately scrape off the worms that would crawl on them. The person assigned to protect me was a little boy about 5 years old. I wasn't confident that he was watching properly, so I was trying to sense any movement I could feel.

I felt a worm just below the neck and between the shoulder blades where I could not reach.

I panicked. "Get that worm off me immediately!" I yelled.

The boy became confused and began to stutter: "What? Where?" He was unsure what to do.

He was obviously not capable of doing his job properly. I was caught in a situation under the supervision of an immature child that would kill me. I thought: *I know everyone bitten by these worms has died, but I will not die.* My hands and feet became numb and it spread quickly through my body. When it got to my heart it would kill me.

I awoke and realized it was a dream. Through it, the Lord was speaking powerfully to me; I had better pay attention to His voice. I prayed and wondered what situation the Lord was warning me about. I cannot place myself under the cover of someone too immature to cover me. It opens the door to the enemy and could be spiritually deadly. The Lord gave me the meaning and we were spared from a trap the enemy had set for us. I marveled! We praised and thanked the Lord for His mercy over us.

He leads us and guides us when He knows we want to walk in the Spirit; He loves us as we love His presence. We need adequate cover for the call we are walking in. Lacking this cover can quench the Holy Spirit within us leading to dryness and deadness. This warning had my attention and brought prayerful discernment to my spirit

The Lord speaks to me powerfully in dreams; it is a way of God's revelation. We walked out the instruction given through the dream. Later we saw what the Lord spared us from, what we didn't understand at the time. We were under immature cover and our life of God within us was in danger. I became more sensitive after this warning.

May this testimony help you pray discerning the happenings in your life. Is the Holy Spirit being quenched in an area you are unaware of? The Lord wants us to have a sensitive conscience in our personal walk, so we can come along side others as the Lord directs us.

The Holy Spirit Leading

The Lord took me there powerfully one day. That evening, I joined my husband visiting a widow woman. It was peaceful as we relaxed together. Minutes after we arrived I heard the quiet voice of the Lord, "Go visit Mary." Mary lived next door. I tried to ignore it and even argued a little: *"I can't do that, it would be rude."* This woman had just given me two books she was reading to look at. I should show interest in the conversation.

My mind was torn as I heard it a second time, "Go visit Mary!" This time a bit louder. Again I argued, *"I have only been here a few minutes and it would be so rude to leave."* I suddenly felt as though the oxygen was sucked from the room; I could hardly breathe. There was lots of air outside, so I jumped up. "I am going to visit Mary," I said and promptly went out the door.

I breathed in the fresh outside air as I approached Mary's door. I prayed, *"Lord, you will have to give me the words for her, because I know she has a house full of people there."* I felt so perplexed. *"Why do I need to visit Mary?"* I prayed, *"none of this makes sense to me."* But I could not disobey the compelling, forceful voice of God.

Welcomed into her home, I joined a circle of people gathered around the fireplace. I continued to pray, *"Lord, you will have to direct me. Mary is in this crowd and I still have no idea why I am here."* I took part in the conversation and commented on a leather love seat in the room.

Mary responded. "Yes, we have a couch that matches this loveseat in the next room. Would you like to see it?"

I chuckled inside. "Sure, I would love to see it!"

So we went to the next room. She closed the glass doors behind us and showed me a couch that I had seen for a couple years. It seemed the Lord was bringing something together, but I had no idea what this was leading to.

"Would you like to sit here in this room?" Mary asked.

"Yes, that's fine with me."

She began telling me about a book she was reading. "It is a beautiful story. This young married couple lived 100 years ago and saw the providing hand of God in their lives."

The Lord put the thought in my mind: *she thinks God only moved a hundred years ago, the enemy has her trapped. Tell her He is moving today. Tell her your story.*

"Yes. God was a wonder working God hundred years ago. But He moves in the hearts of His people today," I began. I felt the power of the Holy Spirit as I shared, "God is so real to me, I would love to tell you how I know Him."

"Oh, yes! Please tell me about God!" she said bursting with excitement. She sat forward with her face as close to mine as she dared.

"We saw a man set free from a murderous spirit a couple of weeks ago," I continued. "We were asked to meet with him as he was dangerous. He told us he was going to murder his brother, his neighbor, the drunk driver that put him in a wheel chair, and his landlord. By the time we left his home he was a different man. He was free and rejoicing."

"Really? That is amazing. Tell me what happened. What did you do?"

"He needed to forgive each one verbally and let them off the hook, but he would not. So my husband told him to repeat the words after him, and he did. He said he felt something leave him as he spoke the words, 'I forgive, I let them off the hook.' He phoned us a couple of days ago and told us he gave testimony in front of his church. He shared that because of this freedom he was now getting married and wanted us to come to the wedding. He was bubbling with joy and praising God for His almighty power."

Mary's mouth hung open stiff in shock. "That is incredible! God is doing stuff like that today?"

"Oh yes, God is amazing, and we need to get to know Him, you will not be disappointed. He is a loving God," I continued.

"Can I just pray about anything," Mary asked.

"Yes, let me tell you how the Lord answered a prayer recently," I responded. "Three years ago my husband and I were at a garden center and I bought a large water fountain for the yard. I finally found someone to deliver it to my home after a year. For another year it laid in my yard and my husband told me to take it to the dump as it was junk. He left on a ministry trip the next day and I prayed and asked the Lord to send someone to put up my fountain for me.

"The very next morning a young man phoned, 'Janet, you do not know me, I got your name from a mutual friend. He told me you may be able to help me find a place to live and a job. I am from British Columbia and I want to move here.' I recalled my prayer and asked, 'Would you like to come out to our place and meet, and I have a fountain you can put up for me. In payment, you can stay in my Bed and Breakfast for two weeks and in that time you should be able to find a place to live and a job.' He was delighted and took up my offer. He found work, but wanted to stay with us longer. He lived with us for the summer and helped us keep up our yard."

I explained he was an answer to my prayer. We called that fountain the "Monument of Prayer." It stands seven feet tall with bright colored lights in the bottom pool. I also gave testimony of how God hears even our small needs; He delights in us coming to Him with our cares.

Two hours later, my husband came into the room.

As he approached Mary nervously stirred not wanting me to leave. He could feel our conversation was intimate and the presence of God was evident. He left the room and closed the door behind him.

A flow of similar testimonies followed. I sensed the Lord wanting me to minister to her and break the confusion the enemy tried to bring through that book. The enemy is so subtle; this book seemed such a sweet story. But when I suggested we should leave as my husband had been waiting patiently, she would hardly let me out the door.

The Evidence of the Power of the Holy Spirit

As we stood at her doorway, she asked, "Janet, I will be in town tomorrow, can we meet at a restaurant so you can tell me more?"

"Sure, I can make that work, call me and we'll set a time."

She phoned early the next morning and we agreed to meet at Ricky's Restaurant at 2:15.

"Janet, where are you, I'm waiting here and can't wait to see you!" It was Mary, calling at 2:00.

"Mary, it's only 2:00 and we agreed on 2:15."

"Yes, I know, but I ran around town as fast as I could, so I'm ready and waiting here for you!"

"Sure, I'll be right there."

With a giant smile and a warm hug she greeted me at the table. The Spirit of God began to flow. I shared many more stories of God's grace with her.

I began, "Our son recently married. I did much of the organizing for this event. Apparently, the most stressful part of organizing a wedding was the mother's dress. So when I went shopping for it, I prayed, 'Lord, direct me to the perfect dress.' I entered a lovely woman's dress shop. I was approached by the clerk. 'I need a dress for my son's wedding,' I told her. 'The mother of the bride is wearing gold color, so I should have something similar.'

"'Okay, I have the dress for you,' she answered. 'Follow me.' I followed her to the back of the store. She handed me the dress. It fit perfectly. I showed my husband and he agreed. 'It's the right dress.' We brought it home and I hung it in my closet.

"A week later I felt deeply troubled. This dress was too beautiful, I would stand out wearing that dress. It was also too much money. I would probably never wear a dress like that again. We could not afford a dress that expensive. But what could I do? My husband had given me this dress. I could not ask if I could return it, he might be offended. I felt despondent. But that day a man phoned to pray with Peter and me.

"When Peter finished the call, he asked, 'is there anything you need prayer for?'

"'Yes, I'm troubled about the dress I have for our son's wedding. I do not have peace.' I told him the story.

"'You seem to be coming against the leading hand of God,' he responded.

"After the conversation I walked up to my bedroom to kneel beside my bed to pray. On the carpet exactly where my knees would go was the receipt for this dress. Marked across the receipt it read 'FINAL SALE.' Complete peace came over me, starting at my head and down to my toes. I saw the Lord wanted to bless me, but I did not know how to receive it, so I repented for arguing with the Lord. He clearly answered my prayer and I was second guessing Him. He graciously taught me to listen and obey."

I shared many more stories. Towards the end of the meeting I went on, "Would you like to hear how I received the gift of tongues?"

She was open to everything I shared. "Yes, tell me about it."

As I told her my story she was amazed. After nearly two hours, we walked to the cash register.

"I hope I did not blow you away with all that I shared," I said.

"No," she exclaimed, "if it would have been anyone else it would have, but I know I can trust what you have to say!" I knew the Holy Spirit was opening that door. If it had been in the flesh she would have questioned what I was saying.

Every Thursday morning for several months, I got a call from her asking to meet again to hear more stories about God. She was hungry and ready to receive more of the Holy Spirit in her life. She later told me the evening I came to her house, she knew I was coming. She went to the window several times, waiting impatiently to see if I was on my way. The Holy Spirit prepared her for my visit. She felt a message burning in me that she needed to hear.

This is my testimony of God using me to bring another of His precious children into a deeper knowledge of the Holy Spirit. The Lord wants this for each of us that know Him. May you be used in this same way. The Lord is calling me to encourage you to walk out this message as well. I give all praise and honor to Him.

End Days: "A New Thing"—A Woman Will Surround a Man

The Lord will create a new thing on earth—a woman will surround a man. (Jer. 31:22)

This verse came alive to me as the Lord directed me to walk through its meaning.

"Peter, if you don't listen to your wife, you will die! These were the first words I spoke to you, and these are the last words I will say to you. Peter, if you don't listen to your wife you will die!" These were the parting words from Donna after spending two weeks with us at a conference in Scotland.

"What do you mean?" Peter responded. I was also on the edge of my seat.

"What you are dealing with is the Jezebel spirit." She went on. "That spirit is the spirit of murder, not only seduction and control. But if it cannot control then it wants to kill."

We both became very attentive and sought further explanation. I only understood such a small part of what I heard. She continued: "You had better listen to what your wife is discerning, or you will die. I've had much experience with this spirit on the Florida coast where I live. It is very strong there. Don't ignore what is happening; you have no idea what you are facing!"

Donna repeated her words several times. "The Jezebel spirit seeks to seduce and control anointed men of God. If she cannot control, she will try murder, she is that angry."

"Thank you Donna," I answered. "Once more I see God's providence bringing you into our path. I marvel how He takes care of His children. He knows every need better than we do."

This conversation scared us both. Peter realized the importance of listening to my discernment, not to be naïve and innocent. The responsibility I carried as the Lord continued to give me revelation and more discernment was sobering. I cried to the Lord more than ever. But the Lord is faithful and miraculously brought people across my path to teach us. This encounter convicted us of the importance of me surrounding my husband so he would be safe. He considered his life in danger and we needed God's revelation to recognize the strategy of the enemy. It drew us together. The Lord wanted us to hear His voice as we walked in unity.

Being a Watchman

My husband loves to feel protected, and in certain situations a woman's discernment provides that. The following incident confirmed his decision to marry me.

After three months of dating it was my birthday. Several of our family members met at a restaurant to celebrate this occasion. I was a legal secretary at the time and was processing divorce papers on the young woman serving us, so I knew this woman well. She was beautiful and I sensed her determined seductive drive. Peter seemed naïve in responding to her actions. It was most obvious to me what was happening as I watched her carefully. When he was cordial with her she put on the charm. When he stopped she became rude.

I watched Peter to see how he responded to this seductive woman. I had become keenly aware of these types of advances after dealing with multiple situations in my life. The next day I decided to pursue his heart and mind on the incident. First, I discussed the situation with another woman who knew this server. She confirmed this woman was very seductive, and she had gone through the same process with her husband. The defining moment came. Peter picked me up from work for lunch. We sat across the table from each other. I wanted to see his eyes clearly.

"What did you think of the waitress in the restaurant on my birthday," I asked, watching his honest eyes closely.

"What waitress?" he responded. "I don't remember her. I was so taken in with you! I don't recall who you are talking about." I could tell he was puzzled. He scarcely remembered her.

"I could tack her hide to the wall," I continued firmly. "I know her quite well, as she is a client at work."

He still looked bewildered. He had no recollection of what took place that night. She was just someone who had served us. Then I explained what I discerned was going on, her advances were obvious. My heart was touched with his naivety and innocence. But I feared my firmness had blown him away. He drove me back to work in silence. The entire afternoon I was preparing myself for his message, "*Well Janet, it has been nice knowing you, but I don't think we are a good match.*" He had experienced an openly expressed firmness in me for the first time, and he was probably in shock. But that was okay with me. I figured that is who I am and I could only express myself and hope he understood me.

By five o'clock I was ready. Now I would find out his response. He walked into my office with a gleaming smile. It caught me by surprise; it was so cute. My heart melted. He seemed even warmer than ever. What was happening?

"How was your afternoon?" I asked as I welcomed him.

"Absolutely wonderful!" he responded. I was somewhat perplexed. What was he thinking? I had been very sharp with him. Was that okay?

We became engaged a couple of weeks later. Then he explained. "That day was truly the defining day. I knew you were the one for me when I saw you were there to protect me, even when I did not know I needed it!"

He felt safe and I felt honored. I respected him and valued his acceptance of my concern. I knew he had eyes for no other woman; he was the one for me. Two months after our engagement we were married. I recognized the importance of building into his life. We avoided time apart doing our own things; rather, we preferred spending our time together. He enjoyed reading so I became an avid reader. I enjoyed snow skiing so he became a good skier. We learned to do what the other enjoyed.

As we began to have children and they reached school age I realized I was the thermometer, carrying the "mercury," as it were, into the home. I kept the temperature, the atmosphere at a proper level. The woman in the home mostly regulates the atmosphere. "If Mama ain't happy, no one is happy." I began to realize the truth of this more and more. She creates the atmosphere with her speech, with the preparation of meals, by the way she sets the table and even the way she decorates the home. These things may seem small but a definite mood is set by what she provides.

Surrounding My Husband: The Nurturing Anointing

The Lord began to open up the Word to me, "a woman will surround a man," teaching me the beginning stages. Then one day I was "blown away!" My husband and I entered the restaurant of the motel we were staying in. A man we knew was sitting at another table. He approached us with a friend he was dining with.

"Hello, I want you to meet this friend of mine," he began. "I need to leave to catch a plane, but perhaps he can remain with you as I leave."

That seemed a little awkward, but we welcomed him to join us as we needed to eat. He told us where he was from and then he paused to look at me.

Pressing his elbows on the table and folding his arms, he leaned towards me and said: "you have the nurturing anointing over your man!"

He stopped and it fell silent. He continued to look at me. I was startled. I sensed my husband beside me would burst out in laughter, but we shared the chuckle inside. What did this stranger see? He had never met me before, and I had voiced only about three words in conversation. That moment I knew what the Lord was teaching me and releasing to me.

We listened as he continued. "The Lord gives me revelation as I walk with Him and he speaks to me often. I work in business but I also have a pastor's heart and provide ministry as the Lord leads me."

The presence of God was there the moment we sat down together. We continued to share for much of the morning. It has been a rich connection for our lives.

I thought about the word "nurture." Webster's Dictionary reads: to nourish; to cherish; to tend; to train; to rear; to bring up. This is the natural inclination of a woman; the way the Lord has wired His girls. But the enemy has come in with the counterfeit: control. When we walk with the nurturing anointing we walk in our God given authority. It brings peace in the home. Control brings confusion and every evil thing. This was such a confirmation and an encouragement to both of us that we were overcomers in our walk with the Lord. It was like a kiss from heaven; what a pleasure to receive that at times! The Lord knows when we need encouragement.

"A woman will surround a man," my husband reminisced. "That's the role you play. I know the Lord has instilled this in you and you've been obedient to this call."

"I praise the Lord for His work in me," I responded. "I've nothing to boast of, it's the Holy Spirit that works this grace within us."

This has been a very important part of our journey with the Lord. Nurturing brings life into the marriage; control brings death. The woman in the home plays a very important role. As we submit to His will and purpose for us, we have sensitivity to His leading.

Carriers of His Glory

Satan fears women whose seed will deliver the fatal blow to his kingdom. Women are "twice refined" and carry God's glory when restored to their God-given positions of effective ministry. God has a plan for these women to arise and shine for the glory of His kingdom.

It is significant that Jesus revealed himself first to women after his resurrection and sent them to tell his other disciples that He had risen. 1 John 3:8 says: "The reason the Son of God appeared was to destroy the devil's work." The devil tries to suppress the voice of the woman. Jesus came to restore her place, authority, dominion, and proper partnership with her husband that Satan distorted in Eden.

This role walked out by a spirit-filled woman, in her right place, walking under anointing is a secret the enemy does not want revealed. The corporate voice of many women gathering together in unity to join cause and purpose releases great power. Especially true in the spirit realm, it is one of the reasons the powers of darkness fear the woman's voice, and tried hard to silence it from the beginning. God made the woman to be a perfect partner for the man so together they might accomplish God's plan. God "custom-built" woman to be an exact, equal, and perfect counterpart to the man. He fashioned Eve from one of Adam's ribs, from his side, which is appropriate for one made to stand by his side as an equal partner. According to Jewish tradition, "The woman came out of man's rib, not from his feet to be walked on; not from his head to be superior, but from his side to be equal; under the arm to be protected, and next to the heart to be loved."

Many times in Scripture God has used women as vessels of His Spirit to lead and direct His people. And where He says, "I will make a helper fit for him," He planned to provide a sharer with him as an equal, in the image of God, and from the same material as the man.

Martha came to Jesus upset that Mary was not helping her serve. Instead of rebuking Mary, Jesus rebuked Martha. That was against the culture of that time. Their duties in the home excluded women from spiritual instruction. He said, "Martha, Martha, you are worried and troubled about many things. But one thing is needed, and Mary has chosen that good part, which will not be taken away from her." Jesus wanted her to join the men as a disciple.

Furthermore, Ephesians 5:15 gives instruction:

> Be very careful, then, how you live—not as unwise but as wise, making the most of every opportunity, because the days are evil. Therefore do not be foolish, but understand what the Lord's will is . . . Submit to one another out of reverence for Christ."

From this I understood the power of working "together," submitting to one another, as iron sharpens iron and two are better than one. This is where unity begins before it can flow into our churches and into our city.

Ephesians 5:22 speaks to wives and husbands:

> Wives, submit to your husband as to the Lord. For the husband is the head of the wife as Christ is the head of the church, his body, of which he is the Savior. Now as the church submits to Christ, so also wives should submit to their husband in everything.

As we women walk under the covering authority of our husbands, there comes a sense of peace. The Lord teaches a rank and line of authority and outside of that there is confusion in the home. There is harmony as we walk according to the principles of God's Word.

Ephesians 5:25 provides instruction for husbands:

> Husbands, love your wives, just as Christ loved the church and gave himself up for her to make her holy, cleansing her by the washing with water through the word, and to present her to himself as a radiant church, without stain or wrinkle or any other blemish, but holy and blameless. In this same way, husbands ought to love their wives as their own bodies. He who loves his wife loves himself.

This explains the cover we have under our husbands as they love us in exactly the same way Christ loves His church. A woman loves to feel protected and our husbands are the provision the Lord has placed over us. We speak life into our husbands as his help-mate, and he provides protection over us as the weaker vessel, each walking together on the same path, playing our proper role. These instructions were written for our benefit by our all wise Creator. Similarly, Jesus prays for all believers in John 17:22:

> I have given them the glory that you gave me, that they may be one as we are one: I in them and you in me. May they be brought to complete unity to let the world know that you sent me and have loved them even as you have loved me.

Walking together in marital unity, we walk strong and in authority, and God commands His blessing. This way we spare our lives from much grief and disappointment. Listening to what the other is sensing daily is a journey for which the Lord continues to give us grace.

From Glory to Glory

God has called us to be carriers of His glory. To arise in this role we can change the atmosphere in a situation and leave a divine impression with the people we meet. In 2 Corinthians 3:18, the Apostle Paul states, "And we, who with unveiled faces all reflect the Lord's glory, are being transformed into his likeness with ever-increasing glory, which comes from the Lord, who is the Spirit."

God's glory—His splendor, His honor, His prevailing power—comes to change us, to make us like Him. In that process of changing from one degree of glory to another, God multiplies the presence of His glory within us. As a result, His glory becomes so evident in our lives that even before we speak about Jesus, they can sense His presence in us. He has overwhelmed us with Himself; we can become God-possessed.

God desires us to carry His presence across the world. As we simply respond and yield to Him, He will release His glory through us to those with whom we come in contact.

Promptings of the Holy Spirit

"We need to join this group gathering in Washington DC from Canada," my husband announced one day. "It is with the Council for National Policies, a high profile right wing think tank."

I was perplexed. We live in Canada and going to a week of US political meetings seemed somewhat senseless.

"Why do we need to go," I asked.

"I don't know, I just sense we need to go."

"You have no idea what we need to go for?"

"No, I just know we need to go."

We packed our bags and drove to the US border.

There, the border guard asked, "What is the purpose of your trip?"

"We're going to the Council for National Policies meeting in Washington DC."

"What? This makes no sense, come inside."

After some questioning they let us go; they were puzzled, as we all were. But the compelling inner voice wouldn't be denied.

We met with the Canadian team and joined the meetings. It turned out the meetings were important. Significant connections were made with people who we introduced to others in our lives. We also built friendships with the team that joined us from the US. The Lord has His ways of connecting kingdom people together.

We have learned to listen to the still small voice that compels us forward even if it seems like a mystery. I question my husband when it does not make sense, but have learned to submit when I don't understand. Before we fully had this worked out in our lives, we faced trouble.

My husband came to me, "the Johnsons want us to meet them at the border. They want to discuss permission for their son to date our daughter."

"Oh, I don't think that will work," I commented. "He's not the one for our daughter."

"What makes you think that?"

"I don't know, I have that sense."

"Well, that's not a good enough explanation to give to the parents."

"I know, but that's all I can say. He's like a son to us, I like him, but he is not the one."

"We cannot say that," concluded Peter. "So let's go and meet with them and release the relationship, they like each other and he seems like a great young man."

I went with Peter, and eventually the conversation turned to the relationship. I said nothing. They began a relationship, but two weeks later it ended. What I sensed in my spirit became obvious even though I couldn't have put it into words at the time. My husband and I took notice from this, and discussed the importance of listening to the sensing we have in our spirit. Often, feeling the way we do does not make sense, but it's God whispering to our spirit.

A few days later, sitting with my husband, I sensed in my spirit, "honey, we need to trade in our car."

"Why? The next miles will be the most economical, I like this car," he responded, clearly not thinking about the discussion. His mind wandered as he flicked his pen.

"I feel it's time to trade it in," I repeated, knowing we were not connecting.

Nothing more was said until I raised it again a month later, "Honey, we need to trade in our car."

He responded the same way. "This car drives so nicely, and the next miles will be the most economical."

We connected no better than the previous time. The next day the transmission started acting up and half an hour later the engine went out. It was totaled.

"You said you were sensing we should trade in our car," my husband recalled, this time attentively. He sat with his head erect and eager.

"I don't know what it was exactly, I just felt we should trade it in, I had no reason. It was just this sense. How do I explain it? There are no words to explain."

This continued happening until we came in tune with the still small voice within us. It took this training to get our attention.

Again my husband came to me, "We need to go to a conference in New York City," he began. "I have been invited by a group of men that I met in Texas."

"Why would we go there if you already got to know them? Why not go again to Texas?" I countered.

"No, I am sensing we need to go to New York."

So, again we flew to this big city for several days, wondering what we needed to learn or do, or who we should meet. On the last day, my husband was walking through the crowd and overheard a couple of sentences that two men were exchanging. He waited until one man left and approached the man that caught his interest.

"Hello, I am Peter," he began with a warm hand shake. "It's good to meet you. What do you do?"

"Hello, I am Jeremy, I'm involved with an environmental project that takes care of waste material."

There was a connection as they spoke. It was the Holy Spirit.

Jeremy said. "I came to this conference because the Lord spoke to me to come and meet the man that I am to work with. I was not to go and find the man; the Lord said he would walk up to me. You are the man."

There was a deep bonding in the Lord. It was God's appointment.

We have learned that the Lord often leads His people this way and we need to be obedient to the still small voice. We have learned to listen to each other when one of us senses God's voice. We also need to discern the voice of the enemy, as he also tries to prompt us. Not every voice is from God.

The Woman's Call: Surround and Nurture

I did further research on the meaning of Jeremiah 31:22. "How long will you go here and there, O faithless daughter? For the Lord has created a new thing in the earth—A woman will encompass a man—(surround a man)." I found this verse declares more than a reversal of the relationship between the woman and the man. The verse uses the Hebrew word neqavah (female, woman). Sabab is the Hebrew verb for "to surround, go around and encircle." Thus the neqavah will "surround" or "enclose" the man. But also means "to turn back, to change, to turn around." This is the next thought of God's word in Jeremiah. In the renewed covenant, the relationship between the man and woman will "turn back" to the original design of God: a woman will come around him, to be his helper.

Looking back to the creation of the woman, God created woman as a helper, an ezer. A similarly pronounced word is the verb azer, which means to gird, primarily for battle. As the original helper, the ezer had a protective role in areas that the man was weak. The complementary dovetailing of respective strength and weaknesses was lost at the fall, which distorted the call to have dominion into a bid for domination.

The word for "man" in Jer. 31:22, is not ish or zakar for man or male. It is geber. This word contains more than a reference to gender, it refers to the nature of man with overtones of spiritual strength or masculinity, based on the verb gabar, meaning to be mighty or great. This is warrior language. The implication is that even the mightiest of men will now find protection and direction from the neqavah. The world will be turned right side up; when God restores the original, the ezer/neqavah will once again be the rescuer, the spiritual director and the one who keeps the man's face before the Lord.

God's original plan for marriage is stated in Genesis 2:24: "For this reason a man will leave his father and mother and be united to his wife, and they will become one flesh." This is the marriage that God intended. The man would leave his previous family connection and cleave to the woman. The man breaks his former relationship and establishes a new exclusive relationship with his wife. Jeremiah 31:22, "A woman will encompass a man," suggests that God has not abandoned His original model.

Proverbs 31:11 reads" "Her husband can trust her, and she will greatly enrich his life. She will not hinder him but help him all her life." (NLT) This word "trust" is not used in any other human relationship, it's usually in reference to trust in God. This word of divine "trust" is applied to the marriage relationship. This verse states that a man "trusts" his wife. The theme of the <u>ezer</u> the helper is evident here. No man will trust his wife as he trusts God, unless he believes he can trust his life to the hands of someone stronger and more capable.

God's original plan created woman as the helper, <u>ezer</u>; that protection and provision, which could not be found elsewhere to meet his needs. The serpent drew this away, and the woman failed to fulfill this divine role. Eve would still bear children, but in sorrow and the man would rule over her, the consequence of sin. But it didn't erase the divine commission. The fall did not erase the objective of God's plan; God's plan for marriage has not changed. We must take God's original intention seriously. His children are called to open the door for God's will to be done on earth, and it needs to shape our marriages.

Thus, a man is to "trust" his wife because it is in his best interest to do so. He does this as his wife models the caretaking effort of God. Her responsibility is to nurture, protect and help in the same way that God nurtures, protects and helps. This may be a new challenge to the woman, it may mean a new mindset. We may need to allow the Word to renew our minds. When I received the word I had the "nurturing anointing" I became eager to further my knowledge in what God was teaching me. He was taking me by the hand and leading me deeper into the truths of God's word. We need to be nurturers of our husbands.

So we read in 1 Peter 3:7 that husbands are to honor their wives:

> In the same way, you husbands must give honor to your wives. Treat her with understanding as you live together. She may be weaker than you are, but she is your equal partner in God's gift of new life. If you don't treat her as you should, your prayers will not be heard." (NLT)

This is very powerful. Honoring is not simply acknowledging and recognizing. Honoring includes voluntary obedience. God knew what He was doing when he directed this order. If this is not walked out, we may as well not pray. How often do we wonder why it seems we pray and nothing happens? The first priority is to order our married relationships aright.

Authority Versus Control

What is the difference between authority and control? Authority welcomes the Holy Spirit, control quenches the Holy Spirit. One brings life to our spirit and the other brings death. Consider the following differences between authority and control.

1. Authority : David   Control: Saul
2. Authority: Gives   Control: Takes
3. Authority: Freedom   Control: Bondage
4. Authority: Lives in a spirit of   Control: Lives in a spirit of
   love   fear
5. Authority: Equips us   Control: Robs us
6. Authority: We rely on God   Control: We rely on others
7. Authority: Raises sons   Control: Raises slaves
8. Authority: We grow   Control: We weaken
9. Authority: We use our   Control: Our weaknesses are
   strengths   exploited
10. Authority: Makes us fly   Control: Smothers us
11. Authority: Justice   Control: Judgment
12. Authority: Will lay down their Control: Will take another's
    life   life

Control is self-centered and works out of selfish ambition. James 3:16–18 instructs us:

For wherever there is jealousy and selfish ambition, there you will find disorder and every kind of evil. But the wisdom that comes from heaven is first of all pure. It is also peace loving, gentle at all times, and willing to yield to others. It is full of mercy and good deeds. It shows no partiality and is always sincere. And those who are peacemakers will plant seeds of peace and reap a harvest of goodness.

Control is domination through our flesh—our sinful nature. The summons to take dominion and authority in the earth is not a call for oppressive domination. Domination is a fleshly substitute for the godly exercise of true, God-ordained authority. We understand what it means to take dominion in the earth in Genesis 1:26:

Then God said, "Let us make man in our image, in our likeness, and let them rule (take dominion) over the fish of the sea and the birds of the air, over the livestock, over all the earth, and over all the creatures that move along the ground.

This is exercising God-ordained authority. God made man in His image and likeness to rule and take dominion over all the earth. How do we take dominion over all the earth? By being filled with the Holy Spirit and releasing the fragrance of Christ where ever we go. His glory will cover our land as "His Bride" releases it.

Praise the Godly Woman

Proverbs describes the wife of noble character in 31:25:

She is clothed with strength and dignity, and she laughs with no fear of the future. When she speaks, her words are wise, and kindness is the rule when she gives instructions. She carefully watches all that goes on in her household and does not have to bear the consequences of laziness. Her children stand and bless her. Her husband praises her.

Are we women our husbands praise? Are we praised for what we do or for who we are? Are we praised because we reflect the character of Christ? The woman who fears the Lord is to be praised! Praise given to a woman that does not fear the Lord can destroy her, by increasing her desire to excel in her own abilities and feeding her pride. Given time, it will lead to a fall.

As we unpack the meaning of <u>ezer</u> we become aware of God's original intention for the woman as helper: to provide the needed protection and provision her husband could not find elsewhere. As women, our responsibility is to nurture, protect and help our husbands in the same way that God nurtures, protects, and helps. We are to discern the traps the enemy has laid for our husbands, leading and guiding them so they do not fall prey.

Many men fall into the arms of seductive women. Our men need to be on guard, but wives are to surround their husbands from such women. Men can be oblivious to the subtle trap these women set. They know this strength they have over men. Particularly, if a man is anointed, women can be driven by the enemy not to give up until he is taken out. As wives, we must be on guard and aware, surrounding our husbands, protecting, and nurturing them. Stand as a watchman on the wall. Guard your man.

Here is a word to women: stand in the position to which you are called; surround your husbands. "He thwarts the plans of the crafty, so that their hands achieve no success" (Job 5:12).

My Call to Speak to You: Take Heart

One Sunday morning our church service was different. The preaching was cut short, and the elder in charge said there would be an announcement. He ushered the lead pastor forward with his wife. To almost everyone's surprise and shock, they announced they were stepping down from ministry! We were perplexed.

As my husband and I stepped into our car we had picked up a little information.

"He has fallen with a woman," my husband began. Our eyes connected with a hollow look of despair. I felt like shouting: "That cannot be!"

"Yes, and I know who it is!" he continued.

"Really? Who?"

"It's Krystal!"

"Oh, yes, that makes sense. That's why she has been acting so strange."

My stomach became sick. Immediately, I began to grieve. I continued to grieve more intensely the next day. The middle of the third day I knew this grieving could not continue or I would collapse. I knew the only thing I could do was talk to the Lord.

I turned to make my way up the stairs, stomped my right foot on the first step and blurted out, "Lord, why am I grieving like this?"

Instantly I heard the reply: "because this is the call on your life!"

Shocked, I stood there not able to move! Every muscle froze. What did that mean?

My grieving stopped and I felt a charge enter my spirit. I knew that moment, the Lord had given me a message and I must release it to God's people. This sin grieves the heart of God. Women, surround your husbands and men listen to your wives. Be a team against the seductive woman. They are a snare.

Ezer also has the sense of "save from danger" and also "deliver from death." This was the word spoken earlier to my husband, "Peter, if you don't listen to your wife you will die." The Lord had to properly align us with Him and with each other to save my husband from danger and deliver him from death. The Jezebel spirit is the spirit of seduction, control, and murder. The Lord taught us graciously step by step as we walked out this part of our life.

His grace is sufficient to walk out His plan. He has given us this promise: "When the storms of life come, the wicked are whirled away, but the godly have a lasting foundation" (Prov. 10:25). As we stand together in our ordained and united position in marriage, we will experience the power of God to keep our lives safe. When the woman surrounds, encompasses, and protects the man, the relationship is restored; a symbolic image of what God will do. What the world considers weak, unequal and less important, God gives a new position: one of power, responsibility and value. This isn't so "new"; it's God's intended structure restored, redeeming the world from the corruption of sin. It's our world that is upside-down. God's created order is the right way up.

CHAPTER 12

A Lovesick Bride of Christ—Our Created Purpose

"The purpose for which you were born was to have this intense romance with Jesus, and out of that will flow your assignment." These words came powerfully from the Holy Spirit as my spirit was delighting in the love of my Bridegroom God.

It began with an unexpected phone call.

"Would you and your wife please come join me," Rachel inquired. "I am in this beautiful resort for several days and would love to have your company."

"Yes!" Peter was enthused. "That would be a wonderful get-away for us. We will join you for two nights."

Our bags were in the car, and we were ready to go.

"Just wait a couple of minutes, I need to make a quick call before we leave," I said as I stepped out of the car.

I dialed Jackie's number.

On hearing my voice Jackie responded, "Janet, I had a dream about you and Peter last night, do you have time for me to share it?"

"Sure, please quickly share."

"I dreamt I walked into this large home and entered the dining room. I saw you and Peter feasting with a group of people. The only other person I recognized was Rachael. I left and joined the children in another room."

"That is a good word, Jackie. We are on our way to a resort to spend three days with Rachael and this tells me we will be feasting at the table of the Lord. Thank you for sharing. That was an encouraging dream."

Overwhelmed, I shared this with my husband as I jumped into the car.

"Can you believe we received this word just as we leave?" I was startled. "I wonder what God has for us these next couple of days!"

"Yes," my husband exclaimed. "I felt we needed to go, it will be exciting to spend time with God."

We arrived and relaxed for the remainder of the evening. After breakfast the next morning, we gathered in the living room.

"I am sensing we need to go through the Song of Solomon," my husband began.

"What? That's the most difficult book for me to understand. Like, my neck is like the tower of David?" I said rolling my fingers up my neck.

"Yes. We'll read it responsively. You and Rachael read where it says Beloved, as that is where you are speaking to Jesus, and I will read where it says Lover. That is where Jesus is speaking to us."

"Ok, that sounds good, let's do that."

I gained a new understanding and a deep hunger as we proceeded through the entire book. We finished, my spirit was refreshed, and I wanted more of what I received. I looked through the many books my husband had packed for our trip. I prayed and asked the Lord which book I should read. "The Pleasures of Loving God" by Mike Bickle stood out. Once I started reading I could not put this book down as it continued to speak to me. Mike saw himself as God's favorite one, a place to which the Lord brought me a couple years previous. I rejoiced.

He described a phone call from a man with this message: "he said that God told him that the Holy Spirit would emphasize the Song of Solomon, releasing its truth throughout the entire church and even to the entire earth in the coming generation." My heart welled up in such gratitude as I entered into the sense of that prophetic word. He states, "I do not know of any book that changes our paradigm of God, line upon line, like the Song of Solomon." I read this minutes after we finished going through the Song of Solomon with such heartfelt devotion.

My spirit was fascinated with His beauty. I fed upon the concept that romanced warriors are protected and empowered. I felt the Holy Spirit wooing me into His presence. "He wants us to be loved and a lover first, and then He wants us to disciple the nations, starting with our families and neighbors." These truths were clear confirmation of what Peter and I had sensed for some time. I was drinking it in. The Holy Spirit came on me with power as I read his quotation from Song of Solomon 5:10–16:

> My beloved is white (radiant) and ruddy, Chief among ten thousand. His head is like the finest gold; His locks are wavy, and black as a raven. His eyes are like doves by the rivers of waters, washed with milk, and fitly set. His cheeks are like a bed of spices, banks of scented herbs. His lips are lilies, dripping liquid myrrh. His hands are rods of gold set with beryl. His body is carved ivory inlaid with sapphires. His legs are pillars of marble set on bases of fine gold. His countenance is like Lebanon, excellent as the cedars. His mouth is most sweet, yes, he is altogether lovely. This is my beloved, and this is my friend, O daughters of Jerusalem!

I read this quote again. It became more intense. I read it a third time. Now it was overpowering. I felt my body would burst. I jumped up and was out on the canal road experiencing this intense love relationship with Jesus, my Bridegroom God. The stream of love was beyond what words could explain. I felt the flow of words written in the Song of Solomon but understood them more in today's thinking. This continued for about forty five minutes. Then as I was returning the words from the Holy Spirit broke in again: "The purpose for which you were born was to have this intense romance with Jesus, and out of that will flow your assignment!"

Immediately, I realized I didn't have to figure out my purpose according to my gifts, by what I was best at, or what I thought was best or most fun. No! I only needed an intimate walk with God and to listen to His voice. Learning this was very important to me. As we surrender our lives to God, only then will God give direction and take us to places we may least expect. I had no idea at that time His assignment would be to write a book about the grace and glory of God! This is most surely God's assignment.

January 20, 2010 was a special day. I entered into that wedding union with Jesus. It was the end of the second seven year period and the beginning of a new era, the era of the "Bride of Christ." I walked out each day of the first seven year period not knowing what the Lord had for me in my journey. But the second seven years stretched me spiritually bringing me into a resting place. I wait to see what the Lord has to teach me in the process of becoming the purified Bride.

The Eyes of His Bride

Overwhelmed with His love, I saw how Jesus is "conquered" by His bride's extravagant love, how our devotion deeply touches His heart. Our minds cannot grasp how all the armies in hell cannot conquer Jesus, but the eyes of His bride "conquer" Him when they remain true to Him in testing. Jesus says in Song of Solomon 6:5: "Turn your eyes from me; they overwhelm me." This is the love I felt coming from my Heavenly Bridegroom.

Mike Bickle emphasizes:

> We become powerful and fearless in the grace of God when the primary purpose of love for which we were created begins to be fulfilled. This is the anointing of the first commandment. And we carry our love as our reward with us wherever we go, even during dry seasons.

Gazing upon the beauty of the Lord was the number one theme of King David's life. In Psalm 27:4 he says: "One thing I have desired of the Lord, that will I seek: that I may dwell in the house of the Lord all the days of my life, to behold the beauty of the Lord, and to inquire in His temple."

The Lord revealed to me the beauty of Jesus, as it holds a powerful place in God's end time strategy. As I see it unfolding, the Father will use the beauty of Jesus at the end of the age to fascinate the end time Church with the love of Jesus. The Bride of Christ sitting at His wedding table is the highest position of honor for all God's creation. He invites us in Revelation 3:20–21:

> Behold, I stand at the door and knock. If anyone hears My voice and opens the door, I will come in to him and dine with him, and he with Me. To him who overcomes I will grant to sit with Me on My throne, as I also overcame and sat down with My Father on His throne.

As Christ and the bride feast at the table, the bride sits with Him in the position of government and authority as well. God has also chosen His bride to teach secrets of the Gospel to the angels.

> To them it was revealed that, not to themselves, but to us they were ministering the things which now have been reported to you through those who have preached the gospel to you by the Holy Spirit sent from heaven—things which angels desire to look into. 1 Peter 1:12.

We have an invitation to Holy Romance as the Holy Spirit invites us to enter into the magnificent love song of a heavenly Bridegroom and His waiting bride. This romance will excite our hearts and give satisfaction that will fill the deep longings within us. This is the real key to the joy of holiness. When God allows the human spirit to see, if only a glimpse, the heavenly Bridegroom, it is the most powerful experience. When God the Spirit releases His revelation to the human spirit, nothing is more beautiful, more powerful, and more penetrating. God wants to communicate this blessed union to us, responding to people who are reaching out to Him. Being "kissed" by the presence of God is sweeter than anything else we could experience. This is what I felt!

Smell of Death versus Fragrance of Life

This flame of Holy Romance will either enrage, or it will ignite a greater love to burn within the people who already know His love. To the one we are the smell of death; to the other, the fragrance of life:

> But thanks be to God, who always leads us in triumphal procession in Christ and through us spreads everywhere the fragrance of the knowledge of him. For we are to God the aroma of Christ among those who are being saved and those who are perishing. To the one we are the smell of death; to the other, the fragrance of life. (2 Corinthians 2:14)

This message came with personal revelation through a dream one night. I was carrying a large sprayer on my back. The sprayer was filled with anointing oil. As I walked along the side of this large building I was to spray a squirt of this oil in each flower box positioned on the ground around the building. The sides of each flower box were approximately twelve inches high and the top curved in about two inches. Thus my view of the soil in each box was not completely visible. The remaining foliage in each box was dead and brittle as winter was approaching. I gave several boxes a squirt, but as I lowered the nozzle into the fifth box, I spotted a very small snake moving along the bottom. Thinking nothing of it, I released the squirt. Immediately a large snake, five inches in diameter came into my face, twelve inches from my nose. I woke ready to scream. The Lord had my attention!

What message did the Lord have in this? As the anointing is released, not everyone will receive it. There will be times the enemy will manifest himself. What seems like a small snake will turn into a monster in a second. It was a warning that I must be ready. I share this testimony for each of God's children. The Lord is so gracious I continue to marvel. I saw the meaning of 2 Corinthians 2:14–16.

I understood same spirits attract, and opposite spirits conflict in spirit realm warfare. This will become more evident as we enter the end times. As the Glory of God falls, those aligned with God will receive His blessing and those who defy God will receive His judgment. This is the spiritual blessing of the outpouring of the Holy Spirit, which will reveal those offended by the work of the Holy Spirit.

We need to be discerning because many that talk about the spirit are not talking about the Holy Spirit. In this conflict we will receive more of the power of God and the outpouring of the Holy Spirit. As we clash with the powers of darkness, but stand in the power of the Holy Spirit against the intense darkness, we will see the greater intensity of His glory. Greater is He that is in me than he that is in the world. All the powers of Hell have no grip on the bride as she walks in union with the Bridegroom.

His Glory Will Cover Our Land

The Lord doesn't want us to just be religious, to dot the i and cross the t according to a particular doctrine or philosophy. He has called us to be lovers, to work in the harvest fields with hearts that are intensely in love with desire for the Lord of the harvest. The Lord is calling his bride to the harvest, to preach Jesus as the passionate Bridegroom.

The presence and power of God will be poured out and cover the earth in the End Times. God's people will enjoy His divine presence, beauty and power in a way we could never imagine. The Glory of God will cover the earth as the waters cover the sea. When the glory is manifested, the nations will look to Jesus Christ, and great multitudes will be saved in the greatest ingathering of souls in the history of mankind.

I contemplated the Lord's promise: "His glory would cover this land." What could this possibly mean? What is the glory? And how will it cover our land? I waited for the Lord to give more meaning through revelation.

As the Word of God revealed understanding of this glory, it became a storehouse of wealth. When we suffer with repentance, we release eternal life; we release the glory of God. But how is the glory going to cover this land? It will happen as God's people understand the truth of God's Word that we must suffer with repentance. Without that, we release eternal death. One or the other will be released from us, greatly magnified in the End Times. The gray areas will be removed, no sitting on the fence. We will either serve the Lord or the enemy: suffering with a heart of submission and love towards God, or with a heart of resentment. When we feel pain, from whatever situation or even for no real reason, and use it to get the attention of the crowd or as a form of control, death is released. I will explain more on this matter in a later chapter. But it needs to be understood by God's people. Ask the Lord for His Spirit to illuminate this message; it is a matter of life and death.

Bridal Warriors

As the Lord began revealing "who I am in Christ," it grew to the point where I felt loved by God more than anyone alive. His love was so strong it seemed no-one else could receive any more. I expressed this to a woman I had never met. She responded, "Wow, I feel the same!" Her understanding excited me. Mike Bickle's book later confirmed what I was feeling. In his introduction, he states:

> I am really beginning to believe that I am one of God's favorites! Now, that may sound arrogant to you until you understand that God has millions of favorites. Through the lens of the passion of His own heart and the gift of righteousness, God sees us as those He loves even as He loves His own Son (see John 15:9; 17:23). This fact makes us God's favorite people, and as I grasp the living reality that He really likes me, then I have a key foundational reality that helps me to enjoy life.

That we are "the favorite one" of God has a depth of understanding. John is to the New Testament what David is to the Old Testament. This unique revelation was given to John of the pleasure God had in him, even though he was weak in the flesh. Jesus Christ had seen John as a lover. We need to see who we are because of Him; this is our identity as a new creation in Christ. The heavenly Bridegroom has chosen us as the delight of His heart: to rule and reign with Him in His expanding empire, and eternally in the Kingdom of God. We are what He longs for, His inheritance. We can never be insignificant; we can live in the glorious revelation of His love. King David was the example of the intense worshiper in the Old Testament. He had deep intimacy with God, a picture of the bridal revelation.

Although my first response to the call to the Song of Solomon was negative, I soon realized the message in this book was a powerful experience with the Lord; a message to see myself through the revelation of the bride of Christ. I had understood the walk of "the warrior," but I know now I will never enter into a more radical position as a warrior than as a bridal warrior, a romanced warrior against the kingdom of darkness. This is where we will be secure, and our heart will be protected. In this posture, we have power to sustain us in the battle. Other warriors will burn out, be injured, not able to endure without this passion burning deep in their hearts. The "romanced warrior's" heart will be protected by experiencing Jesus' love and beauty.

Therefore, the Lord has been waiting for us to mature and to come to the place where we are old enough for love. Then we can enter into a deeper relationship with Him; not just as a Father but also as a Lover, because children have no capacity for romantic love. As children, we learn to know the father heart of God. This is important, but as we grow up, God wants to reveal to us His bridegroom heart. We need to be spiritually old enough to understand bridal love.

> I made you grow like a plant of the field. You grew up and
> developed and became the most beautiful of jewels. . . . Later
> I passed by, and when I looked at you and saw that you were
> old enough for love, I spread the corner of My garment over

146

you and covered your nakedness. I gave you My solemn oath and entered into a covenant with you, declares the Sovereign Lord, and you became Mine," Ezekiel 16:7–8.

The Message version of the Bible concludes this passage with: "and entered the covenant of marriage with you." God is longing for His Church to reach maturity and understand this truth.

The Bridal Season

The five-fold ministry gifts are given to the Body of Christ so that we may be built up, reach unity, and become mature.

> It was he who gave some to be apostles, some to be prophets, some to be evangelists, and some to be pastors and teachers, to prepare God's people for works of service, so that the body of Christ may be built up until we all reach unity in the faith and in the knowledge of the Son of God and become mature, attaining to the whole measure of the fullness of Christ. (Eph. 4:11–13)

The Lord wants to take us into the bridal season. As we mature we are overcomers. There are many promises to the overcomer. We read in Revelation 2 and 3 what will be received:

> To him who overcomes, I will give the right to eat from the tree of life, which is in the paradise of God. (2:7)

> To him who overcomes, I will give some of the hidden manna. (2:17b)

> To him who overcomes and does my will to the end, I will give authority over the nations. (2:26)

> Him who overcomes I will make a pillar in the temple of my God. (3: 12)

> To him who overcomes, I will give the right to sit with me
> on my throne. (3:21)

These are powerful statements from Jesus describing our inheritance—the Lord telling us He desires us to sit with Him on His throne. This is indescribable wealth, riches we cannot fathom with the carnal mind. Again, our purpose for living is to give Him our hearts as voluntary lovers, to be His Bride, to be overcomers, and from that will flow our assignments. God has called us into a place of intimacy and power that is far beyond that of the angels.

As voluntary lovers of God, we love because we see His beauty. We enjoy loving, we long to love, it is not forced obedience, but flows from the spring of living water within us. Developing our relationship with the Bridegroom is the surest way we will know His plan for us. That will change our priorities and set us on course for the life He has for us.

We are identified as "lovers." It is who we are. God wants us to *be* someone before He wants us to *do* something. In our fleshly desire, we want to *do* something in order to *be* someone. God wants us as lovers so we can work for Him. When Mary and Martha were in their conflict, Martha was not wrong; she wanted to serve and do her part. Her priorities were reversed, her natural interests were to work and to serve, before she was a lover. Her work was a distraction. Christ called her to be a lover first, then out of that would flow her assignment. This story is recorded so we will recognize being the lover is the first priority.

God has called me to proclaim the glorious message of His bride to His people. God has promised to send a glorious presence to divinely shelter His people as the storm breaks forth over this earth. This presence is the union of the bride in love with her bridegroom. His glorious presence will become a part of their lifestyle. As God strategically places His people, His power will be upon them. Jesus said: "Most assuredly, I say to you, he who believes in Me, the works that I do he will do also; and greater works than these he will do, because I go to My Father" (John 14:12).

As Jesus went to be with the Father, He promised those who believe in Him would do the same and even greater works than He did. These words are from Jesus Himself. This generation will witness the greatest demonstration of supernatural power ever seen. God describes this generation the most in His Word. This generation has a powerful role to play. We are to "arise and shine, for your light has come, and the glory of the Lord rises upon you. See, darkness covers the earth and thick darkness is over the peoples, but the Lord rises upon you and his glory appears over you" (Is. 60:1–2).

Intercession

I sought the Lord about preparing His Bride for the End Times. What would it look like? What is it to be a Bride? I understood intercession in the light of Luke 18, the cry of the persistent widow. The Lord revealed the perspective of the persistent widow to me. I was at a conference and was picked from the large crowd to come forward, and the very first words that came from the woman of God was, "you are the persistent widow in Luke 18; you will not give up!" This word at that time showed me prophesy is for encouragement.

The next morning, my husband phoned as he was on a ministry trip.

"I am going into a meeting with the president in fifteen minutes and I am going to step down from this ministry. The warfare is too intense."

As he told me the reasons he felt rising inside him, I saw a vision of a little two inch ball on the floor in front of me, it had big eyes and a very large mouth grinning widely as it said: "I have authority over you!"

In a second, I symbolically ground him into the carpet and said, "you have no authority over me, in Jesus name!"

I explained my vision to Peter as he finished talking. I know now those words were anointed, because I did not understand them at the time.

"Peter, you think we are faced with a principality, that is as big as a city. I just saw the enemy and he is only as big as you think he is. You have been called to ministry and you must go forward in the name of Jesus and in the power and might of the Holy Spirit."

The Holy Spirit came on me as I spoke with authority over the darkness overwhelming my husband. I knew I was not speaking on my own, but the Holy Spirit spoke through me giving me confidence and boldness to declare my authority in His name.

The Word is clear in James 4:7: "Therefore submit to God. Resist the devil and he will flee from you." A flood of peace overcame me. My husband felt weak and I needed to stand beside him. The Holy Spirit gives us the authority in the name of Jesus to resist the enemy. We must take that authority over his domain.

My husband went into the meeting with great courage and felt the Lord go before him. After that day we saw God do amazing things. The vice-president told my husband he was used to bring the Holy Spirit into the organization.

Then I remembered the words from the day before. The Lord had given me the persistence of the widow. I gained greater understanding of who God is, and the authority I carry in the name of Jesus. I felt the persistence of the Holy Spirit upon me.

Now I understand intercession as His Bride. To pray from the posture of bridal intimacy is important. Without it, our prayer life will be stunted, and our hearts unsatisfied. Intimacy with Jesus brings forth the fervency we need to pray. Standing in bridal Intercession ("standing in the gap," Ezekiel 22:30) before the Lord God on behalf of others is the essence of intercession. As Jesus is in the presence of God interceding today, so we, as His Bride, are summoned as partners in this labor, in union with Jesus Christ.

CHAPTER 13

Bridal Intercession

God is choosing to draw believers to prayer in a depth of intensity never before experienced on the earth. I believe a new day is dawning in the ministry of intercessory prayer. God has a passion for His people to know His goodness, to seek Him based on the confidence that they learn, and to act on the prayers God births in their hearts.

My earlier prayer life was likened to the persistent widow in Luke 18—"should always pray and never give up." She came to the judge relentlessly asking for her needs to be met. She became a perpetual presence in his court, to the point he used the phrase "she troubles me with her continual coming."

Jesus' intent was not to say with this parable, "Here is what prayer is about and this is the only way to pray." In fact He was saying, "If that kind of appeal by one with no rights or standing is eventually effective, how much more will the prayers of God's beloved Bride be effective with Him whose heart is ravished with love for His Bride?"

God is calling us to realize we appeal to Him in an entirely different mode. We enter into the season of maturing as the Bride of Christ and no longer have the mentality of the widow. God is poised to reveal to us the ravished heart of the Bridegroom.

In the parable of the persistent widow, Jesus leaves a sense that there is a higher way of prayer, a way of approaching intercession that is more effective than the model of this woman. The key to understanding the parable in Luke 18 is in the form of a question Jesus asked the disciples: "When the Son of Man comes, will He find faith in the earth?"

With this question, if the persistent widow would be the model prayer the Lord is promoting, then the interpretation would obviously be that faith is modeled in the persistent widow out of her desperate perspective.

A better definition of faith is one built on a God who is not at all like the unjust judge. Having faith in the true character of God is to stand in constant agreement with God's perspective of reality and to live life according to His principles. I don't form my opinions on what seems evident, but on reality according to His view. Our confidence comes in the still and intimate places of the heart; where the knowledge of the Lord is revealed in the calm and quiet voice of the Lord tenderly wooing His Bride to Himself.

Out of a place of intimacy, true travail is released and we pray the heart of God. From that intimate place arises a true birthing that brings forth the fruit of intimacy.

The time of restoration has come for the Bride. Intercession is at the core of this restoration. The fearful, anxious, problem-centered intercession of the widow will not suffice to accomplish what God has in mind. Only prayers of agreement with God's nature, character and plans, brought to Him by his Bride that is in love, will accomplish what He has purposed; prayers of compassion, born out of intimacy with God.

The evidence of intimacy will come forth when the burden of prayer is unexpected. Many examples are given throughout this book, such as standing in the gap and compassion prayers. My heartfelt prayer is that your understanding will be enlightened and the Bride of Christ will arise and shine for the glory of the Lord has risen upon you. God is calling His Bride to intimacy where prayer flows from God's heart.

Walking in Bridal Intercession

I was praying with an intercessor by phone one morning when I received an incoming call. It was my husband, so I put my friend on hold and took his call. He began to explain a situation in the business that was critical. The numbers in the book keeping needed to come together before five o'clock in order for the business to go 'public' as a publicly traded company.

I suggested I pray together with my friend. As I pushed the button on the phone to connect with her again, the Holy Spirit fell on me with power. I could hardly say "Hello" to her. As I did, she said, "the Holy Spirit just hit me!"

We prayed together and we hung up. Two minutes later she called and exclaimed, "Janet you need to pray in the Spirit, I just saw some streamers as we hung up." I began praying in tongues when the Holy Spirit hit me with such power I wanted to scream. I was praying in the Spirit so loud I felt like I would burst.

My daughter came home to pick me up to drive me to town so I could pick up my vehicle while I continued to pray. During the fifteen minute drive I lost my voice. My husband called me at five and stated, "Everything has come together to become a Publicly Traded Company, we have seen a miracle!"

We realized later, the Lord protected that company while everything else went sideways. It was birthed in prayer.

That was unexpected prayer under the power of God. I did not have control of what was happening and could not stop until the intercession was complete. I give this testimony to glorify God and exalt His name above every other name. As we are emptied of self and filled with Him, the living God, we will see God work and do amazing things.

Bridal Intercession: Standing in the Gap

Called to "stand in the gap" on behalf of the sins and failings of others, became real to me recently. I was with many of my husband's family members to pray specifically for the family. We received revelation to pray against the spirit of religion that grips us in different areas of our life where the Lord wants us to walk in freedom.

"I feel the religious spirit is holding me back," Cheryl began, "I am not effective in witnessing in the university. I don't feel I have a proper heart for my fellow students. I feel critical. It hinders my connection with them. I need prayer."

"Yes, I feel it is keeping me in bondage as well!" Dana added. "I knew there was something that I could not identify, but that's it, the religious spirit! I want to be free!"

"Well, I think it is a spirit that needs to be addressed," Marsha commented. "Let's pray for the whole family."

Prayer began around the circle. The moment I began to pray I sensed I needed to "stand in the gap" for the entire family. I prayed. "Lord, I stand in the gap for the family. I repent and ask forgiveness for opening the door to the religious spirit. I lay this sin at the foot of the cross, and I leave it there with you Jesus. I pray that every door be closed and your Holy Spirit will come and reign in our hearts." At that moment the Holy Spirit came upon me with such intense power my body could not handle it. In shock, I screamed loudly. I had no idea I had a voice with that volume. My dignity in shreds, I groaned for several minutes. I was not sure what took place at that moment, but one thing I knew—it was very real!

Within a couple of weeks we watched as several members of the family were completely transformed. One especially became a completely different person. "I repel the religious spirit today," Bradley exclaimed. "At one time I was in total bondage and had no idea. Wow! I feel a freedom that I never knew before."

Standing in the gap burns in my heart. I have learned the power of it; I learned it the hard way and I know the reality of it. This testimony is hard to deliver but it grips my heart to share with you.

I had a dream that called me to pray for a dear friend of the family. I prayed and also prayed with my husband, but felt no breakthrough. I was puzzled and did not know what to do further. I continued to feel the burden for days. Two weeks later this man died. I was devastated and cried to the Lord to reveal why this happened. After two years I received revelation that I must stand in the gap for people that have open doors in their lives that give the enemy opportunity to kill, steal and destroy. This is the enemy's assignment. We know his strategy.

The day I received that revelation, I was faced with another matter of life and death. I received a text from one of my children. They had received a texted suicide note from a friend. They did not take it seriously, but laughed because it was so out of character for this girl to be saying anything of this nature. As I received this message, I cried out in intercession, standing in the gap, repenting for every sin she had committed, laying every sin at the foot of the cross. I asked the Lord to close every door to the enemy, and to send His guardian angel to protect her and keep her safe. I felt such incredible power in prayer at that moment and I had faith that the Lord heard my desperate plea.

I texted this young woman, but received no answer. But about twenty minutes later, she responded and asked me to come and get her. She was going to commit suicide, and knew the enemy was driving her; she felt a strong presence of evil. Being a person of prayer herself, she knew it was demonic and from the pit of Hell, but the enemy had such a grip on her she lacked the strength to overcome it. She said that she felt the moment I began to pray the power was broken. A man began to yell to her not to do it; she knew the angel of the Lord had appeared.

In Ezekiel the Lord complained: "I looked for a man among them who would build up the wall and stand before me in the gap on behalf of the land so I would not have to destroy it, but I found none" (Ezek. 22:30). "So he said he would destroy them—had not Moses, his chosen one, stood in the breach before him to keep his wrath from destroying them" (Ps. 106:23).

In Exodus 32:11–14, Moses sought the favor of the Lord and pleaded that His fierce anger would not bring disaster on His people, and the Lord relented. Also, recorded for our instruction is the testimony of Nehemiah as he stood in the gap and prayed, "I confess the sins we Israelites, including myself and my father's house, have committed against you . . ." (Neh. 1:6).

This was also evident one day as my husband and I woke one morning. He sensed a stirring in his spirit,

"Good morning, Honey, we need to pray for Randy. He works as the foreman in our business. I feel he needs prayer."

"Yes, we can stand in the gap for him. He is under our cover and it seems he has no power over some sins in his life," I responded.

We began to pray that Saturday morning, standing in the gap and interceding on his behalf. We did not see him over the week-end, but on Monday morning he came to work.

He exclaimed: "Peter, I felt an oppression leave me Saturday morning. I don't know what happened, but I felt different."

Peter immediately phoned me to share this amazing response to standing in the gap for him.

I give this testimony to help you understand the Word of God as He took me on this journey to see firsthand the power of this prayer. My prayer life has never been the same since I saw how it saves lives, physically and spiritually. Standing in the gap has opened access for many people in various bondages, to receive Jesus as their Savior and Lord and bring them into the kingdom. The essence of intercession is praying on behalf of other people. This is what flows from a heart filled with intimacy with Jesus, from "bridal Intercession."

We were born for this purpose: to have this romance love with Jesus so that His passionate heart would be satisfied. Then Jesus will present us to Himself as His perfect counterpart, washed in His blood, fully like Him, and filled with His glorious beauty. We become more like Him as we gaze upon His beauty.

In the context of intimacy with Jesus, and being filled with His Spirit of compassion, we will begin to accompany Him as He manifests himself and brings restoration of all things to the will of the Father, one person at a time.

The Lord's Directing Hand: Prepared as an Earthly Bride

Looking back to my pre-marriage years, I see clearly how the Lord began preparing me, when I was still a young girl, to be the bride for the man I was to marry. God did not bring my husband into my life until that time of preparation was complete. I often wondered why I lived through so many unusual, out of the ordinary situations. Through them, the Lord taught me to be an overcomer in the work place, in my personal life, and in the church. This was all preparation for marriage to my husband.

I see God's gracious hand in my training to be a bride at the proper stage of maturity to match my earthly bridegroom. The Lord prepared me by walking me through many difficulties in the church, backing away from situations where I foresaw trouble ahead. Then the Lord taught me that winning the battle was to "win the heart." This was a challenge I continued to face, but it was the key to overcoming. Throughout my working career before marriage, He lifted me to increasing levels of maturity to be the bride the Lord wished me to be.

As a legal secretary I had my final challenge. I ushered a client into the lawyer's office. Shortly after, I heard shouting in the office and after several minutes the door opened and the client stomped out. I was breathless as the lawyer approached me. His temper exceeded what I thought possible for a professional.

"Janet, I'm sorry for my anger. I don't want to take it out on you!" he said.

I gave him a questioning look. How was I to respond to that announcement? *This apology should have been given to the client. There is no room for anger at work, or at home either,* I thought. *How was I going to tell him that?*

"Why did you get angry?" I began.

Conviction appeared on his face. His eyes softened almost to weeping. He was completely silent, speechless. He had no answer. He waited for me to continue.

"Anger is something we need to control," I continued. "No argument is won with anger. We say things and we do things we regret later. It's important to practice self-control at all times."

He melted and thanked me for the kind words.

Three weeks later I left to prepare for my wedding and marriage. The incident impacted him so deeply he told my father months later he had raised a wonderful and amazing daughter. When I heard that, my only reaction was to thank the Lord for the amazing grace that He had given me. He had molded me and made me ready for marriage. That message from my father was confirmation I was an overcomer and I was drawing from the grace of God. His grace would empower me to bring honor to His name. Because of that preparation we have an exceptional marriage.

Similarly, the Lord takes us through preparation to be the bride of Christ. We need to make ourselves ready. We need to be overcomers. Overcoming is not walking in perfection, but stepping forward and not back.

Jesus' strategy is not simply to invade the earth with overwhelming power and authority, but to woo and win a Bride through gentle persuasion. He wants us to be voluntary lovers. This picture shows how my husband wooed me and won me as no other man could. I had dated several young men, but no one won my heart, and no one could win the heart of my husband. Our desire was for each other. The Lord is pleased with the single eye.

"How beautiful you are, my darling! Oh, how beautiful! Your eyes are doves" (Song of Solomon 1:15). What does it mean to have dove's eyes? Doves can only see one thing at a time; they have a single focus. They also have only one mate in their life time. Jesus is telling us that we are beautiful as we have the eyes of the dove. This picture is significant: He wants us to have a single eye for Him, to have the intimacy of a bride and bridegroom.

The Spirit and the Bride Say "Come"

A friend gave me a music CD shortly after my encounter with Jesus. The first two songs of this CD are so anointed with the bridal message that I could not play these songs for several months without a strong encounter of the Holy Spirit, weeping in the presence of God. The words are written by Julie Meyer entitled Spirit and the Bride

> Behold I am coming quickly
> And My, My reward is with Me
> To give to everyone according to their works,
> According to their works
>
> For I, I am the Beginning
> And I, I am the Ending
> The Alpha and Omega
> The Bright and Morning Star
> The Center of it all
>
> And the Spirit and the Bride say, 'Come'
> And the Spirit and the Bride say, 'Come, Lord Jesus'
>
> For I, I am Alive
> I was dead, but now I am Alive
> And it's forever and forever more, Amen
> And I've got the keys of death
>
> And the Spirit and the Bride say, 'Come'
> And the Spirit and the Bride say, 'Come, Lord Jesus'
>
> And let he who hears say 'Come'
> And let all who are thirsty come
> Whoever desires, let him drink of the water
> Whoever desires, let him drink of the waters of life
> Just Come, Come

The second song was entitled House of Wine:

There's a brand new song arising
In every people, tribe and tongue
Oh, all generations singin'
Come and dine in the House of Wine

So, come in, into my Father's House
The King has, He's set the table and He's
He's poured the Wine
So come, come in into my Father's House
Come and feast at the table and take
Joy in the Wine
Just come and dine in the House of Wine, Ho
Everybody come to the banquet table
Everybody come to the House of Wine

Here I come, Here I come.

Why do we cry "come"? This world is not our home, it will never fill us and satisfy us. It is fleeting. As we experience some aspect of His love, and see the beauty of our Bridegroom, we are awakened and long for its fullness. That's why we cry, "Come, Lord Jesus!"

PART III:
Secrets of the Kingdom of Darkness Revealed

CHAPTER 14

Angel of Light: The War Between the Kingdoms

The call of the Bride is the call to maturity, to become pure and spotless. Through maturity we become discerning.

"But solid food is for the mature, who by constant use have trained themselves to distinguish good from evil," (Hebrews 5:14). This verse is convicting. We need to examine ourselves. Do we discern good from evil? Are we mature, or are we still drinking milk? We cannot remain babies. The Lord is looking for the "mature bride." We must test every spirit in operation. Yes, we must be responsible to test even the spirits operating in the church.

> Dear friends, do not believe every spirit, but test the spirits to
> see whether they are from God, because many false prophets
> have gone out into the world. (1 John 4:1)

This is the foundation to the question, the first words in the first chapter of this book, *"are you ready?"* The Bride is asked this question. Are we becoming ready? The Lord calls us to prepare for this time, a strategic hour in history. We are still babies if we cannot discern good from evil. The Lord tells us to discern the spirits whether they are of God, with this we must also interpret the times.

Jesus spoke to the crowd in Luke 12:54:

> When you see a cloud rising in the west, immediately you say, "It's going to rain," and it does. And when the south wind blows, you say, "It's going to be hot," and it is. Hypocrites! You know how to interpret the appearance of the earth and the sky. How is it that you don't know how to interpret this present time?

Jesus' words to His people are a warning to be responsible. We must not be immature about the present time. "Are you ready?" The Lord Almighty says in Malachi 3:18: "And you will again see the distinction between the righteous and the wicked, between those who serve God and those who do not." The Sovereign Lord declared to the Levite priests, descendants of Zadok, in Ezekiel 44:23, that "They are to teach my people the difference between the holy and the common and show them how to distinguish between the unclean and the clean." The Lord always spoke to His people to discern between right and wrong, between clean and unclean, between good and evil. Maturity in Hebrews 5:14 is discerning between good and evil. We need to have the Word and the Spirit dwelling continually in our hearts to help discern between truth and error!

The Spirit of Discernment

When Solomon could ask for anything he wished, God was pleased when he asked for discernment. The Lord saw his maturity and blessed him with wealth and riches beyond measure. He granted him these because his heart did not desire them; his heart's desire was for wisdom and discernment. Is that our first desire? It needs to be for the hour we live in. We are "*not ready*" if our first cry is not discernment.

When we walk in this wisdom and discernment we do not need to wait for a "word" or "pray" for every action. Rather, He causes us to be mentally sharper because of the empowering of the Holy Spirit. We can fall prey to deception without understanding this. The Lord graciously taught my husband and I this lesson, and we see many people caught in this snare. God's Word is powerful in Ps. 119:97-104:

Oh, how I love your law! I meditate on it all day long.
Your commands make me wiser than my enemies, for they are ever with me.
I have more insight than all my teachers, for I meditate on your statutes.
I have more understanding than the elders, for I obey your precepts.
I have kept my feet from every evil path so that I might obey your word.
I have not departed from your laws, for you yourself have taught me.
How sweet are your words to my taste, sweeter than honey to my mouth!
I gain understanding from your precepts; therefore I hate every wrong path.

The "Angel of Light"

Do we discern the "angel of light"? This is a sobering and important question. What seems right is not always right. The word says Satan's servants masquerade as servants of righteousness. Notice 2 Corinthians 11:14: "And no wonder, for Satan himself masquerades as an angel of light. It is not surprising, then, if his servants masquerade as servants of righteousness. Their end will be what their actions deserve." Do we discern the servants of Satan? Outside of discernment and revelation from God the human mind will not distinguish them.

We have a model of this person in scripture, the most tragic name in history. It is a shocking and sad story. Let's focus on this man. He walked with Jesus, under the anointing of the Son of God. He was one of the disciples Jesus chose to follow Him after spending the night praying to God. "One of those days Jesus went out to a mountainside to pray, and spent the night praying to God. When morning came, he called his disciples to him and chose twelve of them, whom he also designated apostles" (Luke 6:12). The next verse Jesus names each one that He had chosen ". . . and Judas Iscariot, who became a traitor." His was the last name Jesus records to be His disciple. God had elected Judas to be an apostle, not to be a saint. Judas was never regenerated. He was in the kingdom of darkness all along. Judas never believed. "Yet there are some of you who do not believe. For Jesus had known from the beginning which of them did not believe and who would betray him." (John 6:64).

Why would Jesus choose Judas? This is a divine mystery. But the Lord does reveal His mysteries to His people.

> Now to him who is able to establish you by my gospel and the proclamation of Jesus Christ, according to the revelation of the mystery hidden for long ages past, but now revealed and made known through the prophetic writings by the command of the eternal God, so that all nations might believe and obey him—to the only wise God be glory forever through Jesus Christ! Amen. (Rom. 16:25–27)

God wants to establish us according to the revelation of the mystery hidden but now revealed by the command of the eternal God, so that we might glorify Him. The Lord wants to reveal mysteries to us. The word mystery is defined by Webster as "a religious truth that one can know only by revelation." Again in Ephesians 3:2: "Surely you have heard about the administration of God's grace that was given to me for you, that is, the mystery made known to me by revelation . . ."

Revealed mysteries are a revelation by God's grace, the evidence of God's grace over us—His people who have become overcomers, the mature "bride." It is all about God's grace, about being covered by the blood of the lamb. We can take no glory for ourselves. The Lord has entrusted us to be stewards of the mysteries of God, as recorded in 1 Corinthians 4:1: "So then, men ought to regard us as servants of Christ and as those entrusted with the secret things of God." Another version reads "stewards of the mysteries of God."

Deception Discerned

Why did Jesus choose (elect) Judas, after spending the night in prayer with the Father? What are we to learn from the decision of Jesus in this?

1. Jesus and his disciples were a template, a prototype of the New Testament church, and He wants to teach us from this that there will be false brethren amongst us.
2. We cannot hold the leader responsible for choosing leaders under them who turn to be false brethren.
3. Jesus used Judas to train his disciples in discernment. Their discernment will be magnified one hundred fold, because they will no longer go by what the eye sees and the ear hears.
4. Jesus did not expose Judas' deception to the other disciples.

What can we learn from this? Our eyes may see sheep, our ears may hear sheep, but they may be wolves. Therefore discernment and revelation is critical. We must be carriers of the light as we walk before the darkness. Let us walk in the light the Lord has given us, so we will receive more light. Disciples of Christ are ambassadors of Christ. Thus, Jesus wants to train us in discernment so we do not go by sight or hearing, because it can be deceiving. If we do not weigh the spirits, whether they are of God, we will be deceived.

What character did Judas display? What kind of man did he seem to be? He carried the money bag, so he had to be a respected, trusted man. He did a good job in the eyes of men. When Jesus said, "One of you is a devil," none of the disciples suspected Judas. The Scriptures are clear he was never questioned by any of the disciples as to his walk in any way. Apparently, he lived like the most righteous of the group. The others argued seeking status that would make us question them: "where is your heart?" Judas was winsome and influential.

But who was Judas underneath the facade? John 12:6 tells us he was a thief. Judas took advantage of his responsibility to keep the money, stealing from it. Judas loved himself more than he loved Christ. He was filled with covetousness, jealousy, envy and selfish ambition. Let us take heed we do not fall prey to such attitudes James speaks so powerfully against: "For where you have envy and selfish ambition, there you find disorder and every evil practice" (Jas 3:16).

This explains what is under the facade. The surface is not what matters; it's what's in the heart. The mask can cover the heart for just so long; what is really inside will eventually manifest itself. The evil in envy and selfish ambition can be very subtle; and we might have no idea of its working in secret.

Judas also had spiritual gifts. He participated in the miracles, recorded in Luke 10: 17: "The seventy-two returned with joy and said, "Lord, even the demons submit to us in your name." But we know that in the Day of Judgment that that is not a mark of salvation. "Many will say to me on that day, 'Lord, Lord, did we not prophesy in your name, and in your name drive out demons and perform many miracles?' Then I will tell them plainly, 'I never knew you. Away from me, you evildoers!'" (Matt 7:22–23).

Judas also shared in the Lord's Table. He sat with Jesus and His disciples and took the bread and the cup and was judged by the words from 1 Corinthians:

> "Therefore, whoever eats the bread or drinks the cup of the Lord in an unworthy manner will be guilty of sinning against the body and blood of the Lord. A man ought to examine himself before he eats of the bread and drinks of the cup. For anyone who eats and drinks without recognizing the body of the Lord, eats and drinks judgment on himself." (1 Corinthians 11:27–29)

Judas showed remorse for what he did and came back with the 30 pieces of silver. There is a big difference between remorse and repentance. If there is no repentance there is no salvation. Judas never examined his heart. He was exposed to the Holy Spirit but never responded to the Spirit's ministry. "When Judas, who had betrayed him, saw that Jesus was condemned, he was seized with remorse and returned the thirty silver coins to the chief priests and the elders. 'I have sinned,' he said, 'for I have betrayed innocent blood'" (Matt 26:3–5).

There is no salvation in outward morality. The elect sinner is brought to faith from his sin. Judas was in love with his sin. Salvation is free, but it will cost you the world, the flesh, and the devil. No one had more opportunity to be saved than Judas; he had all the teaching, but never examined his heart. No one goes to heaven without genuine repentance of the heart. Judas gave Jesus a kiss as he betrayed him. A kiss shows affection, friendship and intimacy. Compare Judas' kiss in Matthew 26: 48: "Now the betrayer had arranged a signal with them: 'The one I kiss is the man; arrest him.' Going at once to Jesus, Judas said, 'Greetings, Rabbi!' and kissed him."

Demonstrated here is the war between the kingdoms. How subtle. The outward shows affection while murder is in the heart. "Wounds from a friend can be trusted, but an enemy multiplies kisses" (Prov. 27:60). Or from the Amplified Bible: "Faithful are the wounds of a friend, but the kisses of an enemy are lavish and deceitful."

Judas had a hypocritical charade of being righteous. He walked with the anointed Son of God, and the chosen disciples of Jesus, and walked with a pretense of being righteous. He had the form of godliness, but denied its power. "But mark this: There will be terrible times in the last days . . . [people] having a form of godliness, but denying its power" (2 Tim. 3:1–5).

We need awareness and understanding of the war between the two kingdoms. How do we respond to the kingdom of darkness? Can we go into the darkness with a baseball bat to free ourselves? No! What do we do in a dark room? We switch on the light. We need to carry the light; light is stronger than darkness. In a room of light, we cannot turn on a switch to make it dark. But in a dark room we can release light into the darkness and make it flee. The battle is won by releasing the light from the anointing we carry. By suffering with repentance we will dispense eternal life, so that life will be at work in us. As we suffer with repentance the results are eternal life for ourselves and others. Wherever we go, as we release the fragrance of Christ; we dispense life. We will dispense either life or death.

Maturity: We Dispense Light

The assignment of a dispenser of darkness in our midst is to quench the Holy Spirit. As Jesus dispensed light into the darkness, this is what we must do. Darkness cannot rule the light. The spirit of revelation and discernment from the Holy Spirit will lead us as we inquire of Him. The darker the world gets, the brighter our light shines. Our assignment is to discern the spirits, and we can recognize this in a person as we align ourselves with God. Then we are mature disciples, who by constant use have trained themselves to distinguish good from evil.

I had clear confirmation one day about discerning the Spirit on a person.

Robert approached me. "Janet, I want to introduce you to Clarence, he works with me at my office."

I turned to Clarence. "Hello, I am glad to meet you, I know Robert from Toastmasters. I don't know him well."

Robert responded immediately, "We know each other very well!"

His eye brows were raised and his voice was sure. I felt rebuked. I really did know him very well because I felt the Holy Spirit strongly on him, although I had spoken with him very little. At that moment our spirits connected, and we both knew it.

Maturity: Darkness Has No Effect on Us

Why did Jesus not expose Judas as the deceiver, the betrayer? Should we not know these people? Should we not label them and let others know they are dangerous? Judas exposed *himself* over time. Jesus walked in His authority and we need to do the same. Then the Judases in our life will not affect us. We have authority to release light; darkness cannot threaten us.

1 Corinthians 11:19 explains: "For there must be also heresies among you, that they which are approved may be made manifest among you." When darkness appears and makes itself known, it gives light opportunity to show itself. If there was no darkness, light could not be

manifest. We Christians are the light that dispels darkness in our world. Sin cannot continue in the Christian's experience, for light cannot dwell with darkness. Jesus wanted to show forth His majesty and greatness, the darkness of Judas had no effect on Jesus. He did not let Judas disturb him, He called him friend as Judas gave him the betrayal kiss.

The story continues in Matthew 26:50: "Jesus replied, 'Friend, do what you came for.'" Even then, Jesus did not expose Judas. He had no fear of Judas, but called him a friend. Judas could do nothing outside of the will of the Father. Jesus is the light of the world, no darkness can capture him. David predicted Judas' deception in Psalm 41:9: "Even my close friend, whom I trusted, he who shared my bread, has lifted up his heel against me." Then the Holy Spirit spoke in Acts 1:16, fulfilling the prediction of David: "Brothers, the Scripture had to be fulfilled which the Holy Spirit spoke long ago through the mouth of David concerning Judas, who served as guide for those who arrested Jesus . . ."

The plan of Judas, earlier prophesied, was the fulfillment of Scripture. Jesus knew He needed to walk that path in order to redeem His people. He was victorious over death and the grave. Praise and all honor and glory be to His name!

CHAPTER 15

Jezebel Exposed

"Nevertheless, I have this against you: You tolerate that woman Jezebel, who calls herself a prophetess." (Rev. 2:20)

Today, the Lord is saying He has this against us. This should make us take notice of the Word of God to us. Who is Jezebel and what are we tolerating? I will share with you the journey the Lord has taken me on. He surrounded me with the right people when instruction was needed. He gave me numerous dreams of warning, instruction, encouragement, and direction. He has given me the truth of His Word and directed me through several books.

His direction through my experience has shown "exposing" the Jezebel spirit is clearly part of His call on my life. In deep grief at our anointed Pastor's falling, I knew I must speak forth this message in my book. I grieved as Paul grieved, greatly distressed in Acts 17:16: "While Paul was waiting for them in Athens, he was greatly distressed to see that the city was full of idols." Out of my grief, the Lord is calling me to share the revelation He gave me and walked me through. This passion burns within me as I share what the Lord taught me through His powerful revelation. May you receive this warning and take it to heart, because the enemy is very subtle and cunning.

The call on my life to overcome the Jezebel began as a very small child; I was faced with seduction and control even before I began school. The Lord continued to prepare me as a child and I often wondered why

I was faced with such constant challenges. By the grace of God I was able to stand against it and win. For an entire year before I married, I was harassed with seductive phone calls at 2:00 and 2:30 in the morning at least once every week.

During my working period as office manager of an insurance company I was faced with control and seduction similar to what Joseph experienced. Minutes before the office closed, I happened to phone a branch office located several hours south.

In my discussion, one of the girls said: "Janet, we are so excited you are moving here to work on our team."

"What are you talking about, I know nothing about such a move?" I replied.

She continued, "Ryan is coming to move you on Monday and Dave has an apartment rented for you!"

I knew I had been set up for a trap and the only way out was to flee. I couldn't waste any time, as it was Friday night; the heat was on! By the grace of God, I called my boss from my home and said, "I am done today. I will go into the office and pick up all my things tonight. I have another job lined up." He pleaded with me, but I would not walk into the trap that was set for me earlier that day.

The Holy Spirit dwelling within kept me for my husband and overcame the Jezebel spirit in men. My testimony here is to encourage you that God's grace is sufficient to overcome.

A woman ministering in deliverance told me she had never heard of someone overcoming that kind of intensity. Shortly after this session a man spoke into my life with the words, "You first had to overcome the Jezebel in men before you were faced with the Jezebel in women." I found this truth encouraging as it clarified these events in my life.

The Lord wants us to be "skilled" in dealing with the deceit of this spirit. The Lord spoke so forcefully to me one night I was not able to sleep. The word "skilled" came to me for several hours until suddenly my body tightened and I began to shake. The word "skilled" became so loud it was booming in my ears. We need to be skilled to be overcomers. What does it mean to be skilled? We must learn to recognize this spirit of Jezebel and how to overcome it.

We live in victory, not defeat, by opposing this spirit. Recognizing the traits of the Jezebel we walk in our Heavenly Father's authority. We combat her control and seduction, using authority over her control, and the nurturing anointing against her seduction. Walking under our anointing exposes the darkness of the Jezebel as we radiate the light of Christ. This is the epic battle of the end days. The Jezebel hates the authority we carry, especially the protection of a nurturing wife.

Jezebel Quenches the Holy Spirit, Releasing Death

The Jezebel spirit has one master plan: destroy the works and the people of God. Even though the church is her favorite place to be, it is hardly aware that she exists. Yet she is alive and well in virtually most every place believers gather together to some extent. Jezebel has personality characteristics that foster manipulation, control, sexual perversion, and idolatry. The evil spirit that motivated Jezebel's actions remains a widespread influence.

The influence of this spirit is still widespread today. It has always plagued the Church, in an unholy reign among God's people, especially against the anointed people of God. This spirit seems even more entrenched in the Church as it opposes the Spirit of prophecy poured out on all flesh (Joel 2:28).

Startling conclusions can be made about such a woman. My husband worked very closely with a woman for some time. Upon meeting her, even before I introduced myself, I picked up her strong attraction to him and a strange attitude towards me. She wanted to take a picture of him a few minutes after meeting him. He responded by, "Let me get my wife to join me in this picture," and he stepped aside to get me. She had seen us together in the crowd so she knew we were a couple. She was not particularly impressed upon meeting me when I joined my husband, and from that moment displayed a strong resistance to me.

We worked with her for several months, and I continually gave my husband what I discerned about her. It made him very cautious and he kept me aware of everything they discussed. Then one day I said to him: "She draws her strength from you!" This puzzled him, he thought it made no sense. Two days later he had a dream. He dreamt there was a woman sitting by the table with long bushy hair. So much hair it spilled out on the table and filled the table. He noticed her hair and reached out his fingers to touch it gently, but quickly pulled back thinking, *what am I doing?* As he pulled back she looked at him with sweet eyes and said, "It's okay, I draw my strength from you."

He woke startled. He told me the dream. I knew instantly the Lord was speaking to him. He had not understood or completely believed what I had told him about her. A short time later he had another dream that completely revealed the spirit in her, which ended our relationship with her. My husband saw that what seemed innocent was a subtle trap of the enemy. He took it seriously.

Jezebel comes with control, manipulation, flattery and seduction. To seduce, and take out a prophetic leader, a Jezebel spirit will seek to gain favor. She will attempt to unite with a prophetic leader in the realm of the spirit, saying "I'm just like you. I seem to know what you're thinking and feeling. We are kindred spirits." Or she will say, "Nobody understands me like you do," implying that their deep spirituality is beyond what someone else can understand. Then, this "spiritual" tie will attack the prophetic leader's mind, will, and emotions, occasionally displaying itself with sexual manifestations.

This spirit "talks" spiritually, but its strength is born from the power of the flesh, ultimately deadly to the gifts of its prey. The goals of this demonic deceitful spirit are many: to dilute the revelation, to corrupt, defile, instill apathy, and bring disdain of God's true prophetic voice. It seeks to quench the Holy Spirit wherever it goes, releasing eternal death.

Using Flattery to Control

A Jezebel spirit seeks intimacy with power. It may use flattery, fascination and charm in seemingly innocent ways until it gains friendship and confidence, an illegitimate familiarity the prey craves.

As we believers are joined by the Holy Spirit, so the Jezebel spirit seeks to join in soul with others under the guise of spiritual union.

It begins in the realm of the soul. Both men and women will find emotional needs being met by the person carrying this spirit. This often evolves into sexual needs and desires for a male leader. The Jezebel will often pursue for years until she is able to seduce to the point of physical adultery. She is driven and will not give up. "With her enticing speech she caused him to yield, with her flattering lips she seduced him. Immediately he went after her, as an ox goes to slaughter . . . He did not know it would cost his life" (Prov. 7:21–23).

The more men are blinded to Jezebel's identity, the more likely they will fall prey and embrace the "gifted" person. Over time, it becomes more difficult to recognize that this individual operates with the controlling spirit and seeks to conquer and divide. Jezebel often seeks to come between the anointed man and his wife, to bring division in very subtle ways, perhaps making appointments with him alone. The Jezebel uses much grace in her endeavor; a ploy of deceit. She tries to work division in the marriage in order to seduce him with her flattering words. ". . . and flatter others for their own advantage" (Jude 16b).

Beware of Her Releasing

Some individuals with the Jezebel spirit form soul ties by praying and "laying on hands" on a prophetic leader, hoping to impart the seed of its spirit, but are in fact imparting a demonic touch. They often pray beside a prophetic leader ministering to others. They feel compelled to pray for others, but this urge is not of God.

They use flattery to present themselves as a friend with an understanding ear, who knows and understands the pain of being misunderstood and rejected: "yes I understand, like no one else does." They manufacture warmth, enticing the person to become vulnerable and share personal issues. If this person fears rejection, he or she may be blind to a Jezebel spirit that probes this weakness and capitalizes on it, to gain control over him or her. This person's unmet need to be loved has veiled the ability to discern the web of deception being spun.

This spirit must be confronted for its attempts to flatter and seduce, whether the seduction is physical or emotional. When challenged, this spirit usually cowers at first in momentary humility. However, it will eventually redouble its strength and rise like a cobra with intense verbal assault. Such volcanic rage will try to destroy the prophetic voice that confronted them by claiming to be the victim.

The Ploy of "I've Been Hurt"

The Jezebel spirit will never give up when reproved. It will use the "I've been hurt" ploy to be noticed and obtain sympathy from the crowd to regain control; another form of deceit and seduction. Those harboring the Jezebel spirit are lovers of themselves and deceive to dishonor and draw hatred to the anointed person that confronted them. They will not receive reproof. "Do not rebuke a mocker or he will hate you; rebuke a wise man and he will love you" (Proverbs 9:8, the amplified Bible reads "scorner"). The rebuked scorner will not receive it or repent. They will imply you are judging them.

We are to judge only the fruit that is being produced, to judge righteously, to be responsible as a spiritual person to judge all things, and to walk in His presence and be alert to deceptive spirits. May the Holy Spirit lead us into all truth. Do we see the fruit of God's Spirit being portrayed? We must not judge a person's heart or personality or style, only judge the fruit of the Spirit as we see in Galatians 5:22–23: "But the fruit of the Spirit is love, joy, peace, patience, kindness, goodness, faithfulness, gentleness and self-control. Against such things there is no law."

A person is known by the fruit they bear. Are they producing the light of the Kingdom? Is there a walk of humility and repentance, with a teachable spirit? The key is repentance.

"I have given her time to repent of her immorality, but she is unwilling" (Rev. 2:21).

The Lord revealed this to me and gave me the grace to walk it out in prayer. This battle can only be won on our knees. The Holy Spirit gives us discernment to win the battle and favor with the people involved. As God's people with the indwelling Holy Spirit, these evil forces cannot intimidate us as we walk prayerfully against them.

A new tactic of the Jezebel spirit was powerfully revealed to me. My husband and I were attending weekly prayer meetings with the city, and before the meeting began, the leader broke out under the anointing and began to speak, "The Jezebel is covering the land with a new tactic. She is saying "I've been hurt," to bring attention to herself and draw sympathy to control crowds and people." We sat there in utter shock.

I began to tingle and looked at my husband. His eyes showed complete shock and revealed his inner response, *"Can you believe what we are hearing? This is revelation from the throne room of Heaven!"* We were amazed because we were confronted with exactly this. Again, we saw, in this most remarkable way, the amazing hand of God giving us direction and revelation.

Filled with astonishment and wonder I called the woman who voiced this revelation the next day.

"Kamal, would you like to meet me for coffee at Tim Hortons?"

"Sure, I would love to have coffee with you, let's meet at 3:00 this afternoon!"

Before leaving my home, I turned around and paused. I looked across the room to my husband.

"Honey, would you like to come with me, I shouldn't be gone long. If you have time I would like you to join us!"

"Yes, I'll join you."

We entered the restaurant and waited patiently for her to arrive. I wanted to know where she got the information she shared the day before. My heart was burning in anticipation! Did she read it in a book? Did she hear a sermon, a message, a devotional? Had someone told her? Had she received revelation from God? We sat in silence.

Then Kamal arrived. We greeted her and briefly talked about her husband and children. Thinking it would take time to answer my question I wanted to move onto the subject.

"Kamal, last night you explained the new tactic of the Jezebel spirit. You informed us she uses. 'I've been hurt,' to get sympathy and draw attention to herself. She is covering the land and using it for control and recognition. Where did you get that information? Did you read or hear it? Receive a revelation? I have never heard that before!"

"What are you talking about? I do not recall anything you are saying," Kamal responded. "I talked about the Jezebel spirit? I don't know what you are talking about!"

Again, my husband and I were shocked! What? She did not know what she was saying? She knew nothing? How is that possible?

I turned to my husband, "That can only be a revelation from Heaven!"

On the drive home we marveled at how the Lord reveals mysteries through people under His anointing. It was revelation we needed then. Can you marvel with me at who God is? He is a wonder working God. I hope this testimony brings clarity to your life in some way. God brings revelation to His people in many ways.

Addressing the Jezebel

When we reprove a scorner they will hate us. What is a scorner? A person with extreme disdain or contempt, expressing that disdain with disregard and disrespect. This person expresses hatred, a very dangerous person. The Jezebel is the murder spirit. She is driven. We need not fear this spirit as we walk in the power of the Holy Spirit.

Elijah cowered from this spirit and asked the Lord to take him home. I also prayed that prayer when I was initially faced with the Jezebel spirit. It is a powerful spirit that seems impossible to overcome. I wanted to die. I cried out, "Lord, please take me home." Then the Lord taught me to overcome the Jezebel by releasing the Holy Spirit, for God's Spirit is greater than any other spirit. We can walk in authority and overcome any evil spirit that tries to defeat us. Faced with that hatred we must not let it distract us from our walk with God. That is the ploy of the enemy, but as we know who we are in Christ, we do not flinch or give the enemy any place. That spirit has no ruin over us.

Personality Traits of Jezebel:

These traits may vary individually

1. Highlights self
2. Forcefully steers conversations
3. Brags of the hours spent interceding
4. Fears exposure
5. Silences true prophets
6. Excessive jealousy or competitiveness
7. Jezebel appears pious
8. Look at her lifestyle
    a. Personal life screwed up; may be carefully hidden—takes time before exposed
9. Seems genuine, but is spiritually off
10. Jezebel controls the money
11. Establishes authority by controlling
    a. Won't allow others to speak in conversation
    b. Constantly interrupts in order to distract and dominate conversations
    c. Dominates conversations
12. Sometimes she uses a loud voice to interrupt or brag—really subtle ones know this is a dead giveaway and avoid loud talk
13. Uses another's name to gain control or promote her own agenda
14. Plots and carries out destruction of the righteous and innocent
15. Relentless and savage in her relationships and business dealings
16. Quick to anger
17. Anxious, hyper
18. No peace/no joy/frustrated/upset (tries to hide it)
19. Always full of plans, plans, plans; always on the go; looks like she's busy for the Lord

20. Fast talking and nervous (covers up true motivation)
21. Uses seduction to manipulate
22. Jezebel brings a spirit of confusion, division and strife
23. Pretends to be a worshipper and intercessor
24. Jezebel is a backstabber
25. Aligns herself with true prophets to give credence to her agenda

Jezebel's agenda:

1. False prophecy
2. Kill or discredit true prophets
3. Destroy family
4. Brings spirit of slumber
5. Lull people into:
   a. Complacency
   b. Apathy
6. Submission to wickedness
7. Takes control through another (often her husband)
8. Promotes false religion or error in a very subtle way
9. Spirit of murder, rage, hatred
10. Antichrist spirit turns hearts away from true worship
11. Attempts to create focus on herself

Jezebel hates:

1. Prayer
2. Humility, self-control
3. Repentance
4. Faith, peace
5. True prophets and prophecy
6. Truth
7. Manifested fruit of the spirit

Jezebel causes:

1. Fear, timidity, stress, strife
2. Physical weakness
3. Discouragement
4. Guilt
5. Feelings of helplessness
6. Bondage to porn
7. Insatiable sexual desire
8. Holy Spirit to be quenched
9. False accusations
10. Threats
11. Murder
12. Abortion
13. Frustration
14. Moral failure
15. Idolatry

Being on Guard

My husband and I had an ongoing friendship with a couple that came into our lives through the church we were attending. They had a large family and we had much in common. For a lengthy period of time we dined out every Friday night, or she would cook and entertain us. The friendship seemed wholesome from the surface, until it came to a test.

One day my husband was to fly out of an airport a two hour drive away from our home. She was aware of his flight and asked him if she could ride with him as she had a flight from the same airport two hours later. My husband immediately called me after his phone call from her and asked me what he should do.

I responded, "It's okay, let me handle it."

I immediately called her and said, "This won't work, as my husband cannot be seen with another woman riding with him. If you stopped at a gas station, it would take only one person seeing him with a woman and a rumor could start and circulate."

I thought she would receive and understand our concern easily. I know how I would respond to a woman's similar explanation to me. I would feel the love and protection of the woman's response and I assumed this woman would feel the same, but that was not the case.

She exploded with offense. "Who do you think I am? Do you not trust me?"

I responded: "It has nothing to do with you, it has everything to do with my husband. He needs to keep his reputation pure."

Consequently, our relationship went sideways from the moment she took offense. She became bitter. I had small indications she was trying to get my husband's attention, and had told him to be careful, but I had no idea she was driven to that degree. We knew then she was a dangerous woman. A couple of years later we received word that she had left her husband and her beautiful large family. She moved in with an anointed worship leader who was married to a very anointed intercessor. Previously, this couple had been powerfully used in the church.

I praise the Lord for the spirit of discernment, and I pray it may increase in our lives. We are in a time that evil spirits are increasing in their power and we must manifest more of the Holy Spirit's presence. Walking in God's empowering grace, keeping our hearts clean from bitterness, unforgiveness, pride, and other sins will guard against deception.

Control Reigns in a Subtle Way

John Paul Jackson's book, *Unmasking the Jezebel Spirit*, was recommended to me by a man with a strong prophetic gift. I see now the Lord provided this book to answer many questions arising in my mind.

After reading it I handed it to my husband. "Here honey, I wrote you a book, I wrote every word in this book!" I was amazed. It literally explained everything I had experienced.

I saw flattery as a primary tool being used by a person influenced by the Jezebel spirit. Flattery is often used to pry open a door to win hearts to move to a higher level, to seek promotion by church leadership. Although offering sincere compliments that edify others in the Body of Christ are good, flattery differs in its motive. Flattery is looking for recognition and approval from those in authority. This spirit is subtle and only gives in order to get, stealing favor and authority that rightfully belongs to someone else. It moves to take a position to be acknowledged and take control.

Many leaders believe that a person with a strong prophetic gift automatically have the same level of moral character. This can be misleading. A person operating with a Jezebel spirit can portray a very real and even awesome prophetic gift, but be extremely weak in moral character, or in error or weak with their theology. Flattery will transcend and smooth over any differences between people when guided by a sophisticated Jezebel spirit. This spirit seeks to quench the Holy Spirit, using flattery to portray admiration with a motive to control. Flattery will seem to endorse vision and direction and speak the same language as leaders, but only with a motive to gain position and control.

The Jezebel not only seeks to gain position in the church she is attending, but also in other moves of God outside of her church. Such as prayer meetings, Bible Studies, ministries or crusades where God is moving with the Holy Spirit. The Jezebel spirit wants to abort the move of God. If we are unaware of Satan's devices we will be trapped and wonder why the presence of God in our life is not the same as it once was.

An individual with a Jezebel spirit seeks to join other people in the Body who move in the spiritual realm. They realize a spiritual person is looked on favorably and they want to share that favor by working in strategic affiliation. This individual will campaign to win growing influence.

Scripture gives an example of strategic affiliation when the apostles Paul and Silas were on their way to pray and a woman with a Jezebel spirit joined them. She was insinuating that she was also going to prayer by walking beside them. She was hoping to win the acceptance of Paul and Silas and those that watched. She also proclaimed they were servants of God (Acts 16:16). Pretending to be an intercessor, she attempted to gain a spiritual foothold in the city. Paul discerned her motives and delivered the woman of a spirit of divination. This demonic spirit strategically tried to acquire a deeper foothold of influence in the region.

Someone with a Jezebel spirit often seeks to join intercessory groups. This person will try to control the direction and content of prayer. It's only a matter of time before this person will take up leadership. Most of the time the Jezebel spirit premeditates her efforts, but there are times when they may be unaware of how their power works. Whether it is knowingly or unknowingly, the driving force is a demonic spirit.

It is not unusual, as this individual attempts to take over, for the current prayer leader to experience sudden or prolonged health problems or mental confusion and resign. Then the individual with a Jezebel spirit begins to counterfeit true prayer leadership, using false humility and mock timidity to position themselves. Eventually, that disappears and they begin to declare brazenly that he or she knows the mind of God and tell everyone how they should pray.

Often the energy given to prayer will seem to increase. Things seem to get better to those that are undiscerning. However, this energy will begin to dissipate. The reason? Energy derived from soulish passion will not live long. Only that which is born of the Spirit of God will be maintained and lasting and bear fruit that will remain.

If no one has discernment and the Jezebel spirit is left to operate, the intercessory group will end. One-by-one, they will be drained and the desire to pray will be over. The group will begin to dwindle. Then the watchmen in God's house will be scattered and the church is no longer protected. A demonic take over occurs. This is the ploy of the enemy to quench the Holy Spirit within the Body. A spiritual chill develops and few notice it happening.

These individuals will carry false burdens from the Lord, trying to appear very spiritual. They may even believe they are speaking God's words, not being able to recognize the deep deception they are operating under. Once this person gains an open door to the anointed man or woman of God, most often the Jezebel will flood them with "revelation" that has supposedly been received from the Lord. Each situation will have a subtly manipulated scheme to draw attention to them rather than to the Lord. As the roots of this spirit take deep hold in the person's soul; the Holy Spirit, the voice of the Lord and the fruits of righteousness eventually become non-existent.

False Humility

Once a person with a Jezebel spirit receives recognition, they initially respond with false humility. This is only a ploy to further entrap and convince of their spirituality. This misleading meekness will be short lived. False humility is only a mask for deeply rooted pride, arrogance, and deception. They often speak out their focus on humility only to deceive, wanting to exhibit their humility. It is a false, subtle trap of deception.

When this person with a Jezebel spirit is promoted to leadership, they will try to impress on everyone that they are more spiritual than most. Maybe receiving recognition through much learning. They try to make others feel less spiritual and intimidate them. This is a ploy to create an emotional dependency in others, and to lean on the Jezebel's spirituality. They do not sense the deception that is taking place without discernment.

New believers or weak Christians are especially taken in with the subtle power of the spirit of intimidation. Once a person is under the power and grip of the Jezebel it is difficult to remove themselves.

When the Jezebel spirit is within the church, although the church has been given many prophetic words, God's promises never come to pass due to the deception of this dark spirit.

Different Levels of the Jezebel: Receiving Revelation

Many well-meaning believers who operate in a Jezebel spirit need revelation and perhaps counsel or deliverance to walk away from the error. Perhaps, this spirit has not matured in their life. However, other individuals may resemble the mature Jezebel spirit we read about in Scripture. Usually these people do not know the Lord. They join a church to deliberately destroy it through occult means.

Intercessors seek for restoration and building up of the people and things of God. A Jezebel spirit only seeks to unravel and destroy the things of God. We need to be aware of the enemy's smokescreen and be discerning as this spirit is very strong and very subtle.

Do you feel overwhelmed trying to understanding who the Jezebel is? The Lord hears the cries of His people. He will lead us into all truth. The Lord continues to send the prophetic voice into my life to teach me, He also speaks clearly through dreams, of which I have had hundreds. Much revelation has also come as I speak in tongues and one of our daughters has had a strong gift of interpretation. I learned there is a difference between speaking in tongues and praying in tongues. When I speak it is a flow of prophetic revelation, unraveling the strategy of the enemy. When I pray in tongues, I am interceding to the Father in prayer. Speaking in tongues has given us pages of revelation regarding the Jezebel spirit.

Trophies for the Enemy

I had a most intense dream regarding this spirit. In this dream, I walked into a Jezebel woman's home and her husband had hair down his back, immaculately cut and styled. I was taken down to the basement and was shown my bedroom. There were two pure white couches in this room, but containing deeply soiled stains. I was then invited into a room specifically set up and run by two young girls. They explained that the woman was their employer, and she brought in sperm from men she had under her influence of deception, from which they grew leaves as trophies for the enemy. The leaves looked like heavy rubber plant leaves. They showed me leaves that were six feet by two feet in size, trophies for this Jezebel woman. They told me the names of the men she had gathered the sperm from. The dream shook me up. After I told my husband, I lost my voice and could not speak for several days.

There are many stages of the Jezebel spirit; most are not full blown. Some operate in control and manipulation only, others adding the spirit of seduction and flattery. The final stage is divination. Here witchcraft connects with the principalities of the nation and even other nations, and may even entail casting spells.

Casting Spells

Several years ago an intercessor who was part of our team became so stirred in her spirit she could not work. She was so troubled all she could do was pray for my husband and me. Finally we were asked to come together with the four of us and pray. This woman kept receiving: "someone is casting spells on you," which lay heavy on her for days. The very next day a couple came to our home for supper. After dining, we went to the living room to recline. Before the wife sat down she looked at me and said, "someone is casting spells on you." The next day I called an intercessor to pray as was my weekly practice, and she also said "someone is casting spells on you."

The following day at a prayer meeting in our business, one of the intercessors walked in very troubled. During the meeting she kept saying, "we really need to be praying for Peter and Janet." After the meeting she lingered after everyone left to talk to me.

She said, "I don't know what is happening, but something is wrong. We just really need to pray. What is it?"

I replied. "We had reports for the last three days that someone is casting spells on us. Is that what you sense?'

She just exploded. "Yes! That's it; someone is casting spells on you!" By this time we both felt we had received the message. It was clear, someone was casting spells on us.

This stage of the Jezebel spirit takes concentrated warfare because she is ruthless and demonic. But through this the Lord teaches us. We have no choice but to learn how to be "skilled" for war.

Revelation While in a Trance

One day, while receiving revelation on a Jezebel spirit that was operating in the lesser degree of control and seduction, I went into a trance. I walked into the living room and as I sat down the power of the Holy Spirit hit me and I had this vision.

My wedding day would be in two weeks. This wedding was going to be perfect, everything was to be the most spectacular. Seven bridesmaids would wear royal purple dresses. The top part of each was fitted, as was the bottom. But the bottom also had an overlay of delicate chiffon. It would lay in a complete circle, flowing softly over the top of the skirt. They were the most gorgeous bridesmaid dresses I have ever seen.

I called all my bridesmaids to come, with their dresses on, for the rehearsal. The wedding was only two weeks away. The first three bridesmaids came in and they looked spectacular. But the next one had dried mud all over the delicate chiffon on her dress. I told her it would be absolutely unacceptable for this special day.

She argued with me. "I can't wash this dress, it will ruin it, it's so delicate that washing would only wreck it."

I responded, "No. If you take it to the dry cleaners, they'll not only clean it but also press it, and your dress will be more beautiful than the others."

She continued to argue and an unrealistic fear gripped her that it was not possible to clean the dress. I told her that if her dress was not clean she could not be my bridesmaid. I left this choice with her. During this trance I was buzzing and shaking. I shared it with different ones that day, and every time my whole body would shake and buzz, the power of God was so strong.

This is a message to the women that are carriers of the Jezebel spirit that need to be free. There is a wedding day coming that we need to appear as the "spotless" bride. We cannot be carriers of any of this earth's mud and soil. We do not have to put our dresses in our own washing machine. If we do, they will certainly be ruined. But if we take our soiled garments to Jesus, to the foot of the cross, for His cleansing, we will come out more beautiful and spotless as Jesus desires. It is a cleansing beyond anything we can do.

From this trance I felt the Lord calling me to share with the Jezebels that they need to be cleansed from this spirit that is afflicting them. The mud on their garments must be removed; we cannot be part of the wedding feast with dirt on our garments.

Wanting Restoration

We, in the body of Christ, need to support those who have repented from using the Jezebel spirit, to continue taking new steps forward. They need encouragement to continually renew their minds, learning to recognize and adopt God's way of looking at things, and promote activities that restore feelings of self-worth. Servanthood, with healthy boundaries, is a key to restoration, but serving others should not be confused with having authority. Giving them authority at this early stage would be like giving an alcoholic a drink. All areas of rebellion will need to be addressed and amends will need to be made in an attitude of humility, closing the door to the enemy.

Right handling of an attack by a Jezebel spirit will ultimately strengthen a person, or a church. God uses the fiery battles of life to train, strengthen, and refine us (1 Peter 4:12–19). Small battles produce small victories, but great battles produce great victories in our lives.

I feel the testimony of God's grace and glory well up inside of me as I reminisce on the leading of the Lord, His guiding and protecting hand over my life; how He led me through His word, through dreams, through prophetic revelation, and constantly sending people with prophetic words. The Lord often sent people to pray over me unexpectedly.

The Cover of Prayer and the Grace of God

During a counseling course I was attending, we took three days at a resort at the end of the session to wrap up the course. During one of the breaks a man from the class came to me and said the Lord gave him a message for me. He sensed someone trying to take me out of ministry, and the Lord wanted him to lay hands on me and pray protection over me. We were to ask another man to join us. We went to another room to pray. As he laid hands on me he said he felt the ground shake. He had never felt anything like that in his life. The other man looked at me and said, "I cannot tell you what I saw I can only tell you: you will be walking on water and you must keep your eyes on Jesus or you will sink!"

It was a very powerful time of prayer. I walked back upstairs and marveled how neither of these men knew anything about my life, but the Lord spoke so clearly to them. It was a time of need, even more than I sensed. The Lord knew better than me. He protected me and my family from the cruel devices of the enemy and prepared our hands for war.

My testimony is all about the grace of God; His grace has proven to be sufficient for my every need. His grace has empowered me. He just gives more grace in abundance. I don't know where I would be outside of the grace of God. When I see the Jezebel going about using her tactics to promote herself, I think, *there go I except by the grace of God!* Only by His grace do I differ.

It is with this understanding that the Lord wants me to proclaim His grace and glory. It is all about my risen Lord. I cannot take any glory for what God has done. He has made me who I am. He has taken me by the hand as His little daughter and brought me into the resting place at His feet. He will not give His glory to another. With power the Lord spoke to me out of Isaiah:

> "I am the Lord; that is my name! I will not give my glory to another or my praise to idols. See, the former things have taken place, and new things have taken place, and new things I declare; before they spring into being I announce them to you." (Is. 42:8)

This was so powerful I wept deeply, and my spirit yearned several times that day, especially for "I will not give my glory to another." With that I received Psalm 25:14: "The Lord confides in those who fear him; he makes his covenant known to them."

Shortly after that my husband had a dream with the same message. "Do not take the glory!" It shook him to the core. The Lord wants to be magnified in our lives; His name is to be lifted up. As John Newton proclaimed, "Amazing grace, how sweet the sound, that saved a wretch like me. I once was lost, but now I'm found. Was blind, but now I see!" His grace is truly amazing.

CHAPTER 16

Witchcraft

"How can there be peace," Jehu replied, "as long as all the idolatry and witchcraft of your mother Jezebel abound?"

There is no peace with witchcraft. We must be aware and discern this spirit and know its power and subtlety. God's people need to be set free from this entrapment and snare. The Lord says in Micah 5:12, "I will destroy your witchcraft and you will no longer cast spells." The Lord does not want us enslaved by witchcraft but rather to walk in freedom; He came to set the captives free.

In the woe to Nineveh in Nahum 3:4, the city's destruction was, ". . . all because of the wanton lust of a harlot, alluring, the mistress of sorceries, who enslaved nations by her prostitution and peoples by her witchcraft." Then the Lord adds that He is against this and records the judgment for these acts. Witchcraft quenches the Holy Spirit and the work of God. It can abort the move of God. The Lord is preparing our fingers for war, for us to be aware of the strategies of the enemy so he doesn't gain a foothold in our lives.

My husband and I were invited to attend a service where a man was brought in from Argentina to speak to our city. He has a strong anointing and has been part of the powerful move of God in Argentina that began approximately in 1984. Peter Wagner wrote an article "The Awesome Argentina Revival." He writes a section on Spiritual Warfare:

What is the secret behind such effective ministry among the urban masses? The answer to such a question must not be oversimplified. All church growth is a complex interweaving of sets of contextual factors, institutional factors and spiritual factors. Much of what is happening in Argentina can be explained by well-known contextual and institutional church growth principles. I do not believe, however, that they can adequately account for the sheer magnitude of the phenomena I am describing. My personal conclusion is that spiritual factors, particularly power evangelism and spiritual warfare, are paramount.

I agree with Larry Lea who says, "The devil's work is to blind the minds of men and women. It is our work to pray that the power of darkness be pushed back from shrouding people's minds." Powerful intercessory prayer is the chief weapon of spiritual warfare on all levels.

The powers of darkness are evident through the revelation the Lord releases to us. As this man from Argentina came to speak into our city he began to give his testimony at this service. I was amazed at his message, and I surely concurred with him. He stated:

> We had a woman in our church that seemed to be so extremely spiritual, always talking about the spirit. She moved into a high position in our church as she impressed the people with her spiritual talk. Always talking about the spirit. Until there came a day we realized it was not the 'Holy Spirit' she was talking about. At that point we realized we had a witch in our church.

What? I thought. *This is the word this man is bringing us for our city? This man knows the power of darkness. He has walked through much in the revival! He is confirming the revelation the Lord has given me!*

Do we understand the subtleness of witchcraft? Do we think witchcraft is only in Argentina and Africa? This message is for us to awake from our slumber. Pray for revelation for what is happening in our churches. We may be as shocked as this man. Let's not be sleeping in this hour!

Sometime later we attended a conference several hours north. This conference was for one week and had various speakers. A couple days into the conference I sensed numerous witches in the crowd as we drove up to the conference center.

I commented to my husband, "Do you think the speaker is aware there are witches in this crowd?"

"I wouldn't be surprised if he sensed that," he responded.

"If he senses it, what do you think he'll do?" I was curious.

Well, we certainly found out. He was minutes into his speaking and he addressed them. "We have several witches in our crowd tonight. I want you to know I know you are here. The power of God is our strength and no power of the enemy has any right in this place."

As he spoke these words I gasped and glanced at my husband.

"Wow, praise the Lord," I whispered. My voice whispered but my heart shouted!

"You got your answer," My husband responded. "That's what he does!"

How Witches Gain Authority

Visiting Paraguay with my husband and several others for a couple of weeks was a further eye opener. We spent some time with the local people.

In conversation with one of the women I asked, "do you have much witchcraft happening here?"

She responded, "Oh, yes, we sure do. There are many people that operate in deliverance here. They need to be so discerning because witches come to them for deliverance only to invite seven times more demons into them. That is how they get their power."

I was shocked. "Is there any evidence indicating what a witch looks like or acts like?"

"No, not at all, there is no way you would know except through revelation and discernment. Witchcraft is very subtle."

"Wow," I reacted, "We surely need discernment and Holy Spirit revelation when people come for deliverance. We cannot be naïve and receive everyone who comes forward and seems honest and pure in their motives."

I was so stirred I could not wait to explain this to my husband. It is amazing how the Lord leads us to the right places at the right times for more revelation. The Lord wants to train our hands for war. He is so gracious and loving.

We came home with a message that gave us much more awareness and left a lasting impression. People in other countries are aware of witchcraft and I felt convicted at the state of our country. Intercessory prayer is the chief weapon of this kind of spiritual warfare. We need to be praying that the power of darkness will be revealed and be repelled from clouding our minds. Witchcraft opposes the work of the Holy Spirit to stop the move of God. Do not be ignorant of Satan's devices. We need to discern good from evil (Heb. 5:14):

> When an evil spirit comes out of a man, it goes through arid places seeking rest and does not find it. Then it says, 'I will return to the house I left.' When it arrives, it finds the house unoccupied, swept clean and put in order. Then it goes and takes with it seven other spirits more wicked than itself, and they go in and live there. And the final condition of that man is worse than the first. That is how it will be with this wicked generation. (Matt 12:43–45)

The Jezebel Blocks Those Coming to the Feast

I had a powerful dream later that continues to stir me, where I was in the top level of a five story building looking across a room. The room was filled with round tables set for a banquet, with white table cloths and chairs to accommodate ten to twelve people at each table. Everything was prepared for a very large feast, there was no end wall, only tables as far as I could see.

I looked out the window and could see a large parking lot which was completely empty, not one vehicle in sight. As I peered in the distance it became evident there was a person standing at the parking entrance. It was not a greeter I was looking at, but someone turning people away. There was a blockage stopping people from coming to the feast. I knew it was a Jezebel woman.

On my way down to the fourth floor, I saw another room filled with round tables as far as I could see, but no one in sight. Again, I looked outside to the parking entrance while I walked to the third floor, and the same person was still at the entrance blocking people from coming.

I proceeded to go to the second level. There I saw large stainless steel warming dishes with lids as large as four feet by six feet. I took up the lids one by one to see hors d'oevres that were fully cooked and needed to be served very soon or they would be spoilt. I looked outside once more as I went down to ground level. On the ground floor I also saw warming dishes as far as I could see, every one hot and ready to be served. This floor had the main meal with many dishes of various foods that would serve many different nationalities.

Now I nearly panicked, seeing massive amounts of food that needed to be served immediately but no one there to eat it.

This dream shook me badly and as I woke I knew it was a real warning. The Jezebel and witchcraft are stopping people from coming to the feast the Lord has prepared for us. The feast is "ready" and no one is there. Jesus has a table set for us to come to His banqueting table, for His banner over us is love. We are called to come to feast with Him. Come, for His table is ready. There is no time to spare! The food is prepared; don't delay! Come to the banqueting table where He has prepared a feast and is waiting for each one of His people. There is room and food beyond sight. Come today; come now!

Purging Jezebel from our Midst

The parable of the wedding banquet is recorded in Matthew 22. The feast was prepared and the call went out to "come." The call is going out today. Let's not delay. The feast is waiting and is "ready."

This dream was a warning that witchcraft and the Jezebel spirit needs to be removed so God's people can come to the banqueting table. The Jezebel hinders the move of God. We must be discerning and overcome the Jezebel and witchcraft. It is now we need the revelation of God to endure; to be in tune with God's voice. Do not fear as we serve the greater power. His grace and mercy will strengthen us as we lean upon Him. The God of peace will surround us.

Understand that as we overcome Jezebel, we receive great authority! I struggled before the Lord how to overcome Jezebel, seeking the answer from many people to this question. Always the answer was: "do not let them control you and put them out of your life." I never felt satisfied with this answer, and only as the Lord walked me through revelation has the answer come. Releasing the power of the Holy Spirit and walking in the authority of Christ, the Jezebel will cower and be defeated. The Holy Spirit is more powerful than any demonic spirit. Our victor is Jesus Christ, and His eyes of blazing fire will purge Jezebel from our midst. This brings freedom into our lives so we can overcome. We are victorious through Christ Jesus our Lord!

CHAPTER 17

Exposing a Deep Secret of Satan

> To you who do not hold to her teaching and have not learned Satan's so called deep secrets (I will not impose any other burden on you): Only hold on to what you have until I come. (Rev. 2:24–25)

Satan has deep secrets. They are revealed to God's people through revelation; his strategies exposed in God's perfect timing. Satan's schemes are always subtle, never obvious. Without revelation we will be oblivious to their nature. However, the apostle John states that believers can overcome Satan when "the word of God abides in you" (1 John 2:14). When Jesus was tempted by Satan, He quoted Scripture to him (Matt. 4:1–10).

In addition, Paul tells us that the sword of the Spirit, which is the Word of God, is our offensive weapon against Satan (Eph. 6:13–17). In the parable of the sower, Jesus said that there were those who heard the word of God, but failed to take it in, like seed that fell by the side of the road, and so were led astray by the devil.

The Bible gives believers the following instructions about resisting the devil:

Submit therefore to God. Resist the devil and he will flee
from you. (Jas. 4:7)

Take up the shield of faith, with which you can extinguish
all the flaming arrows of the evil one. (Eph. 6:16)

Be of sober spirit, be alert. Your adversary, the devil, prowls
around like a roaring lion, seeking whom he can devour.
But resist him, firm in your faith, knowing that the same
experiences of suffering are being accomplished by your
brethren who are in the world. (1 Peter 5:8–9)

What is the deep secret of Satan? He is our enemy. He has a secret he
does not want us to know! This secret is preceded by Revelation 2:18–19:

To the angel of the church in Thyatira write:

These are the words of the Son of God, whose eyes are
like blazing fire and whose feet are like burnished bronze.
I know your deeds, your love and faith, your service and
perseverance, and that you are now doing more than you
did at first.

Then in verse 20 we hear the warning: "Nevertheless, I have this
against you: You tolerate that woman Jezebel, who calls herself a
prophetess . . ." Then in verse 24, we find the teaching of the Jezebel, the
teaching of Satan's deep secrets with which she ensnares God's people.
Her teaching is: "It is so deep!" Yes, it is a deep secret, but it is a secret
from Satan. It is a snare. She says, "It is so deep, it is all about pain and
hurt!" It is "I've been hurt!" Then as people fall prey to this voice, they
become crippled and death begins to reign in their spirits. Satan does
not want his secrets revealed as he brings death.

As the Lord gave revelation, I was sitting under a message by our lead
pastor covering the message to the church in Thyatira. He concentrated
on verses 18–25, beginning with "Nevertheless, I have this against you:
You tolerate that woman Jezebel." As he read verse 25, he followed with

these words that helped complete the revelation I was receiving at an earlier point:

> She is misleading. She calls herself a leader, but she is teaching the opposite. She is unwilling to repent, saying her teaching is so "deep." To those who overcome her false teaching, what does Jesus say? "I will give you authority over the nations," v. 24, just as He has received authority from the cross.

As I heard those words they completed the picture the Lord was revealing to me. The Lord had revealed the Jezebel speaking out "I've been hurt," using it to manipulate and control and attract the attention to herself. I recognized this as a new form of control, but now I saw its source. Satan has many deep secrets, but in our time, this one needs to be exposed.

The word of God came alive to me in Romans 8: 17. "Now if we are children, then we are heirs—heirs of God and co-heirs with Christ, if indeed we share in his sufferings in order that we may also share in his glory." Then I saw what gives us such episodes of His glory, His presence revealed, His majesty flowing upon us, what brings us this joy unspeakable and full of glory. We pass the test in suffering when we suffer for the name of Christ. God is pleased at our heart's response in obedience to follow Him, whatever the cost. It brings the glory of God; particularly that it will bring the glory to cover our land. As we receive the glory, we release the glory until it fills the whole earth. When the Lord gave me this promise it was a mystery. But the Lord began to reveal the mystery and I became overwhelmed; I just want to share it with all of God's people.

Seeing His Glory Because We Suffer

"Mine eyes have seen the glory of the Lord." There are many worship songs speaking about his glory. This glory overwhelmed me when playing the piano and singing 'Be Exalted, O God." His presence covered me as I started the second half of the song:

> Be exalted, O God, above the heavens,
> Let Thy glory be over all the earth.
> Be exalted, O God, above the heavens,
> Let Thy glory be over all the earth.

Let's also look at the rich promise in Romans 8: 18–21:

> I consider that our present sufferings are not worth comparing
> with the glory that will be revealed in us. The creation waits
> in eager expectation for the sons of God to be revealed . . .
> in hope that the creation itself will be liberated from its
> bondage to decay and brought into the glorious freedom of
> the children of God.

Thus, we no longer consider the suffering we went through in order to have the joy of His glory. I compare it to giving birth to a child. I remember being in labor with our first child. I really thought I would die. But recalling that women go through much pain in giving birth, I consoled myself by thinking, *this is what all women go through. But, I thought: I will never go through this again, I want many children, but we will adopt our children, there is no way I can ever go through this again.* I held this precious daughter in my arms, I forgot everything I experienced, and I was soon expecting the next. I never looked back or even feared as I knew the second child would come. The joy I experienced was so overwhelming I hardly thought about the pain.

I recalled the revelation from 2 Corinthians 4:12 earlier, where the Lord showed me the depth of riches that suffering with repentance brings. Going through this experience, we release eternal life: "So then, death is at work in us, but life is at work in you," NIV. The NKJV makes it even clearer: "So we live in the face of death, but it has resulted in eternal life for you."

It is so important how we receive suffering. We live in the face of death, in the face of suffering, but the result is releasing eternal life to others. How we suffer determines whether we release life or death.

2 Corinthians 7:10 brought me more understanding. Note the clarity the following translations bring:

Preparing the Bride of Christ For His Return

Godly sorrow brings repentance that leads to salvation and leaves no regret, but worldly sorrow brings death, (NIV)

For the kind of sorrow God wants us to experience leads us away from sin and results in salvation. There's no regret for that kind of sorrow. But worldly sorrow, which lacks repentance, results in spiritual death, (KJV)

For godly grief and the pain God is permitted to direct, produce a repentance that leads and contributes to salvation and deliverance from evil, and it never brings regret; but worldly grief (the hopeless sorrow that is characteristic of the pagan world) is deadly—breeding and ending in death. But worldly sorrow, which lacks repentance, results in spiritual death. (Amplified Bible)

The last rendering from the Amplified Bible gives a clear interpretation. The Lord wants us to release life through godly sorrow in repentance. The enemy opposes that; he wants us to have worldly sorrow which results in spiritual death. Worldly sorrow: "I've been hurt," contains no repentance; it is rooted in rebellion and self-pity, in turn rooted in pride and arrogance, self-centeredness and unrighteous character. But it is used in a very subtle way. It grieves the Lord if we fall prey to the ploy of Satan when someone cries trying to gain sympathy by a demonic spirit of Satan.

The Riches of Suffering

The whole Bible gives meaning to us when we understand the richness of suffering. Note what suffering is all about in Romans 5:3–4: "Not only so, but we also rejoice in our sufferings, because we know that suffering produces perseverance, perseverance, character; and character, hope." The Lord uses suffering to mold us and make us into His image; suffering produces the character of Christ in us.

James 5: 7–11 extends the message to "patience" in suffering:

203

> Be patient, then, brothers, until the Lord's coming. See how the farmer waits for the land to yield its valuable crop and how patient he is for the autumn and spring rains. You too, be patient and stand firm, because the Lord's coming is near. Don't grumble against each other, brothers, or you will be judged. The judge is standing at the door.

> Brothers, as an example of patience in the face of suffering, take the prophets who spoke in the name of the Lord. As you know, we consider blessed those who have persevered. You have heard of Job's perseverance and have seen what the Lord finally brought about. The Lord is full of compassion and mercy.

We see Job's perseverance through suffering and the character that was molded in him. As we endure suffering, considering it from the hand of our Lord, we appreciate the last sentence of James' passage: "The Lord is full of compassion and mercy." Can we sing as Paul and Silas did in prison? Their suffering in repentance brought the joy of the Lord on them so intensely they hardly felt their pain. Suffering with repentance brings the Holy Spirit upon us so we can then release it to others. Some will receive it and some will not. To some it is the savor of life unto life, and to others it is the savor of death.

> But thanks be to God, who always leads us in triumphal procession in Christ and through us spreads everywhere the fragrance of the knowledge of him. For we are to God the aroma of Christ among those who are being saved and those who are perishing. To the one we are the smell of death; to the other, the fragrance of life. (2 Cor. 2:14–16)

The NLT version, makes it even clearer:

> But thank God! He has made us his captives and continues to lead us along in Christ's triumphal procession. Now he uses us to spread the knowledge of Christ everywhere, like fragrance rising up to God. But this fragrance is perceived

differently by those who are being saved and by those who are perishing. To those who are perishing, we are a dreadful smell of death and doom. But to those who are being saved, we are a life-giving perfume. And who is adequate for such a task as this?

This is a sobering message. Would not everyone want to receive light and life? Why would anyone want darkness and death? By nature our eyes are blinded. We have a responsibility to come to the Savior empty handed and look to Him. As the brazen serpent was lifted up in the wilderness and those who looked at it lived, so we are responsible to LOOK UP AND LIVE, and not to follow darkness.

Even Christ Jesus, our Lord, "learned obedience from what he suffered and, once made perfect, he became the source of eternal salvation for all who obey Him" (Heb. 5·8). We are called to follow in the steps of Christ's suffering, to endure even under unjust suffering, as Peter explains:

> For it is commendable if a man bears up under the pain of unjust suffering, because he is conscious of God. But how is it to your credit if you receive a beating for doing wrong and endure it? But if you suffer for doing good and endure it, this is commendable before God. To this you were called, because Christ suffered for you, leaving you an example, that you should follow in his steps. (1 Peter 2:19–21)

Who Is Our Master?

Now comes the critical question, "WHO IS OUR MASTER?" Do we suffer with repentance and walk in the glory of our Lord, or do we display the 'deep' secrets of Satan and walk with the spirit that releases death: "I'VE BEEN HURT!" This is the critical revelation that the Lord has given to me. "My people are lost for lack of knowledge"; may each and every eye be opened to the truth of God's word and be victorious.

The Lord is calling His Bride in this hour to make herself ready. This is truly a strategic hour, a sobering time. Be watchful and vigilant. Be alert, at peace and rest in the Fathers arms, watching and waiting on God. Let us be in the shelter of the Almighty and arise and shine, for the glory of the Lord is on His Bride. We need not fear but rejoice for His redemption draws near. Praise, honor and glorify His name.

Who is our Master? How do we suffer? Let us encourage one another to serve God in Spirit and in truth. I need the body of Christ, and we need one another to walk out what God has for each of us. Let us not separate ourselves from the body:

> He who willfully separates and estranges himself [from God and man] seeks his own desire and pretext to break out against all wise and sound judgment. (Prov. 18: 1 Amp. Bible)

> A man who isolates himself seeks his own desires; He rages against all wise judgment. (NKJV)

Let us love one another for love is from God, mature as His bride together, and be strong in the Lord. By His empowering grace we will endure to the end and bring glory to His name!

CHAPTER 18

Bringing Restoration

God wants to reveal His glory through our lives. He wants to build stature and strength in his people for what He is about to do. He wants to pour out the Holy Spirit. In Joel, we see the preparation before the Holy Spirit is poured out on all flesh.

> I will repay you for the years the locusts have eaten—the great locusts and the young locust, the other locusts and the locust swarm—my great army that I sent among you. (Joel 2:25)

Restoration comes first. He begins to restore what the locust has eaten, to replace what the thief stole. This restoration releases the outpouring of the Holy Spirit. He has anointed us with His Spirit to restore:

> The Spirit of the Sovereign Lord is on me, because the Lord has anointed me to preach good news to the poor. He has sent me to bind up the brokenhearted, to proclaim freedom for the captives and release from darkness for the prisoners, to proclaim the year of the Lord's favor and the day of vengeance of our God, to comfort all who mourn, and provide for those who grieve in Zion—to bestow on them a crown of beauty instead of ashes, the oil of gladness instead of mourning, and a garment of praise instead of a spirit of

despair. They will be called oaks of righteousness, a planting
of the Lord for the display of his splendor. (Isaiah 61:1–3)

Bringing restoration, walking in freedom and setting the captives
free is what the Word of God teaches for our lives. We are called to bring
restoration by healing our hearts and healing and cleansing our land.
The following testimonies show where the Lord has taken my husband
and I in our journey with the Lord, helping others walk in freedom.
I hope and pray this will encourage you to walk this out yourself and
help others walk in freedom and glorify the Lord.

I don't believe a Christian can be possessed by the devil. However, I
do believe a Christian can need deliverance from a demonic stronghold
or a particular demonic spirit. Jesus asked Peter how Satan had found
entrance into his heart. This shows that even Peter believed and followed
Christ, but was influenced by a demonic presence.

The Lord makes a way for His people to be set free and healed from
the wounds caused by the enemy's deception. The fullness of salvation is
a process; it's called sanctification. Often a person has a deep wounding
of the past. Wrong habit patterns are built into a person's life, even
demonic structures. Habits and structures must be broken so that the
"new creature" is able to live according to the Spirit and not according
to the old nature. In Galatians 5:16, Paul said, "I say, live by the Spirit,
and you will not gratify the desires of the sinful nature." And "continue
to work out your salvation with fear and trembling . . ." (Phil. 2:12).

Jesus not only gives us eternal life, but a way to be set free and healed
from the wounds of the past so we can remain in the fullness of life
that Jesus provided. The process of sanctification is a continual process.

A Christian can never be possessed by a demon or by the devil,
but can indeed be harassed by demons. There is where the spiritual
warfare of Ephesians 6 comes in. We read in Mark 16:17, "And these
signs will accompany those who believe. In my name they will drive out
demons . . ." This is the desire of the Lord for our lives.

It is such a joy to me to watch God's children being set free from
strongholds and walking in freedom. My husband and I take each other

through deliverance whenever we feel the oppression on us. Then I feel like a new person.

The following testimonies are of freedom being brought into the lives of God's children that were bound in bondage but are rejoicing in the freedom God wants us to walk in:

Testimony from Danielle

I had been miserable ever since I became ill at fifteen. By twenty-one, I had found the words to explain my despair: "I feel like I'm buried alive in a locked steel coffin far below ground, under layers of concrete barriers." I felt silenced, isolated. I tried to understand the barrier and fought to free myself of it for all those years. All that remained of my energy and motivation was a simple determination to keep praying and thinking and trying, whether it got me anywhere or not.

A bondage seemed to control my life to some degree, spiritually, physically, and emotionally. The physical fatigue, depression, and discouragement came to define me. Eventually, I no longer remembered what it felt like to be energetic and interested. Satan was laughing at me. Did he know why God's promises to me weren't happening? I don't know, but I know he enjoyed watching it. I was aware of an evil presence in my room and in my home, which I tried to cast out in Jesus' name, but somehow it kept returning.

I was sick, and no one knew why. Every part of my body was having problems, and no diet, supplement, or change of lifestyle helped. So I spent several years mostly in bed, trying not to be bored.

God had big plans for my life; I knew that. They just weren't happening. I sensed a spiritual wasteland in my life. I knew God would turn it into a garden of fountains, but I didn't know when. There appeared to be a disconnect between my relationship with God and any outflow of that into my physical reality. This was more than a test or a challenge to overcome, this was a bondage to break, a barrier to smash through.

One day a friend mentioned Peter and Janet Van Hierden. She said they were people who, by the Holy Spirit, could discern spiritual realities. I am also quite aware of the spiritual realm, so we arranged to meet them. Within minutes of entering their home, I was explaining my illness, my despair, and my overwhelming boredom with the emptiness and futility of my life.

Peter said, "It sounds like you could use some deliverance!"

Deliverance? I wanted deliverance, but I felt like laughing. One word was not a big enough solution for the extent of my problems. But I gave it a shot anyway. I wasn't entirely sure what would change. Unsure of the power of deliverance, I just gave it to God and decided to wait and see.

Over the next year, my life changed completely. My illness disappeared, my personality changed, I made too many new friends to count, the demons left my room, I developed courage and confidence, and I learned and experienced God's power in my physical reality. Through the incredible, magnificent power of Jesus' blood, Satan is no longer laughing; I am! I don't yet know exactly where God is taking me, but I know I'm headed in the right direction.

My prayer is that this book of my testimony may be helpful for you to know God more intimately. My testimony is not about me, but only to glorify God as Father, Son and Holy Spirit.

> "God forbid that I should boast except in the cross of our Lord Jesus Christ. . . ." (Gal. 6:14)
>
> *Danielle Grisnich*

Testimony from Heather and David

In 2006 we became aware that there were strongholds in a number of offices in our company. We felt these strongholds were impeding certain areas of the business. In our accounting department, a fierce spirit of control caused constant fighting, challenging us as owners. It was disorganized, my husband's assistant talked back to him. In the shop at the back of the building, the guys used bad language, gossiped, etc. We knew we needed deliverance from what we sensed were demonic strongholds. It was affecting the work flow, staff were agitated, fighting.

We invited Peter and Janet Van Hierden to come to our offices and began to pray over our offices in all departments, claiming the blood of Jesus over all of them, and praying down the strongholds we felt in certain offices. Since doing that we have begun to see attitudes change, joy, and unity. God removed some individuals (cleaned His house) from our offices, and we have a peace that prevails over our offices. The strongholds have left and the wind of the Holy Spirit blows through our building.

We continue to pray over the land and the offices. When we added a 4,000 square foot addition to our existing office space, we had prayer over the land and placed a time capsule with God's word in it and placed it in the cement foundation to be the foundation or cornerstone of the offices.

We have seen God restore those areas where there were serious issues and release the company to its destiny: to become the company God has called it to be in our community and city.

The business has grown four times the size it was when we began to pray a cleansing and deliverance over it. We have people on payroll who come once every three months and pray a deliverance of any strongholds over us as a family, the business, its offices, and land. They also pray daily for us and our families/staff/office/business outside the office. The Lord has expanded our tent pegs, and given us favor that we could have never imagined, it is truly a God thing.

We rejoice in the freedom God has given us through healing our hearts and our land and offices, continually praying deliverance over one another and our families and business when we sense a stronghold.

If my people, who are called by my name, will humble themselves and pray and seek my face and turn from their wicked ways, then will I hear from heaven and will heal their land. (2 Chron. 7:14–15). WOW! What a promise. Now my eyes will be open and my ears attentive to the prayers offered in this place. He has heard our cries; what a faithful God we serve.

Heather and David Peddie

Testimony from Katrina

Being married and raising four beautiful sons has brought much joy into my life. It also comes with its challenges, but I continually thank the Lord for where He has brought me, strengthened me and taught me on my journey.

As a family we attend a church where we see God moving among His people and sit under good teaching as well as additional instruction on "who we are in Christ" and "healing of the heart." Along with this teaching, I was privileged to attend the classes Janet Van Hierden was instructing using Beth Moore's material on going deeper with God. After one of these classes I was preparing to go home when, sensing that I had something heavy on my mind, Janet encouraged me to talk and I burst into tears.

A few weeks earlier I had discovered I was expecting my fifth child. I was certainly happy to be pregnant but at the same time I began to be gripped with fear of another miscarriage. About 6 years previous, I went through a terrible miscarriage at ten weeks gestation that put me in the hospital. The fear of thinking I may have to experience that again was crippling me, bringing anxiety and devastation. As I began to weep, Janet came around me, graciously took me to her office and let me pour out my heart.

She immediately detected the fear and anxiety and encouraged me that prayer was important. She started by asking me to confess and repent for allowing the spirit of fear and anxiety to take root in me. I asked forgiveness for opening the door to the enemy and asked that that door would be closed so that the enemy would no longer have that access in my life. Then as she laid her hands on me and began to pray blessing over me. A real sense of peace invaded my spirit and I felt joy beginning to well up inside me. There seemed to be such power and a presence of the Holy Spirit on us as we spent time together.

After praying she mentioned a flow of the Holy Spirit coming upon her and released from her finger tips. I knew something had happened and I felt like a different person. The peace of God flooded me as I left and continued throughout the remainder of my pregnancy. I had no more fear or anxiety about having another miscarriage. I knew that God had a perfect plan for my life as well as that of my unborn baby. I now understood that the strategy the enemy had for my life could be cut off and I didn't need to live my life under his control and domain. Janet's helpful instruction with our prayer time together changed my life.

It brought me to understand spiritual warfare at a new level. I now know the enemy has an assignment to kill, steal and destroy the promises of God, but through healing and deliverance we have the authority in Jesus name to come against the enemy and stop his plans and assignments. Janet has been trained in formal education, but seeing it walked out in the power of the Holy Spirit is what brings reality into our lives.

From that moment my pregnancy went as normal with absolutely no more fear or anxiety and I now have five beautiful sons that the Lord has given me. I am overjoyed to see the preserving hand of God and how God works in the lives of His people. I want to share this with you so you can walk in the understanding of the ways of God. May all the glory go to Him as He is worthy of our praise.

Katrina Roos

Testimony from Marie

I was adopted, raised in a home where I felt I was continually bad and punished. As a young girl I was put into a foster home, and began a life of drugs. I got pregnant at age 17 and watched my daughter being taken in and out of my home most of her life. I was in unhealthy relationships and suffered much abuse mentally, physically and emotionally. But my addiction to crack cocaine and other drugs held me captive in these relationships and I was living on the edge of life. My drug addiction carried on for 17 years and then the unthinkable happened. My boyfriend, best friend, and father to my youngest daughter was killed in a single vehicle accident as the result of drinking and driving. My world was torn apart.

I gave my heart to the Lord and started serving him wholeheartedly and as time went on my pain was not as intense. God then blessed me with a husband and we married August 14, 2010. We entered a Godly marriage and declared our love for each other and for Christ, and that he would be the center of our home. December 2011, my husband left me after I had found out he was back on drugs as he was also a recovering drug addict. Then not long after my daughter who was 17 at the time left me as well.

During this time all hell broke loose, my husband was screaming and yelling at me he was not godly, my daughter took me to court with claims I had beaten her. I could not take anymore, I literally thought I should put myself in the hospital. All I ever felt was useless, bad, crazy and devalued by the people I love the most. Worse yet I believed that I was always being punished by God and I believed he was mean. How could a good God who loves me so much let me suffer at the hands of my family, I was done.

A mutual friend phoned Peter and Janet and suggested to me I go to see them as they do ministry called "healing of the heart." I had nothing to lose I was that messed up. The first time I arrived I was warmly welcomed and loved and God began to do a work in me through this ministry. As I started to go to more sessions it became very apparent that I felt I deserved what I got and believed I was bad. As you can tell from my testimony a lot of bondage comes from this sort of lifestyle and it was deep stuff. I truly believed I was being punished by God and that he did not love me.

As we began to spend quiet time with the Lord asking him to reveal the areas in my life that needed healing, I was amazed at the revelations and insight God revealed through Peter and Janet. It was bang on. As we walked through the healing process the question that I was asked more often was: "Marie, where was God when you were suffering?" As we waited on the Lord he showed me incredible things then I knew he was right there with me through all the bad and that he loved me so much he sent his angels to watch guard over me. I allowed God to heal my heart and fill it with his love.

Since then my husband has come home and our relationship is stronger than ever, my daughter came home and has left me again. This time I know that it is not because I am bad or being punished. Healing of the heart is a very important step to walk out and be able to walk into the full freedom and deliverance God has for you. I know God wants to bless many through this ministry.

Marie Kunz

Testimony from Peter

When I got married to my beautiful bride anything seemed possible for us. What I never thought possible was that 11 years into our marriage my frightened wife would have to move out of our family home, with our three children, to seek the safety of a friend's house after a weekend of angry outbursts.

One morning our Pastor shared with me in his office that my wife was leaving a cycle of abuse that we were living in together. Our pastor clearly showed me the historical patterns and increasing level of abuse; which, unless stopped, would progressively get worse until it would ultimately end in a mass murder-suicide where the entire family winds up dead. As I listened I was stunned and deeply saddened. He said that we we're not near this point but that the cycle of abuse we were in could end up going that far. This was God's BIG wake up call to me. I saw so clearly what I had become apart from Him. My heart broke apart inside and I cried.

I started clinical counseling for my anger and control problems. As I learned how to manage my anger it made me aware of the way I was operating in negative patterns of thinking, self-talk, and fear based control. This was a beginning, but God wanted me to go deeper than the surface.

As this was all happening I was attending our church conference, which was truly a God appointment. I connected with Peter Van Hierden and after some conversation he invited me to the cell group he and his wife were leading. Knowing about spiritual strongholds and deliverance ministry I sought out "Healing of the Heart" with Peter and Janet. They have been trained extensively in this type of ministry, which brings deliverance and freedom from the bondage of the enemy in our lives.

In our first ministry time together Janet shared with me how suffering with repentance brings the Holy Spirit, who helps us to become more like Jesus. Then the Holy Spirit fills us with the glory of God, so that wherever we go, the glory of God goes with us. That took some time to sink in, but I began right away to repent in my mourning for all of the sins God brought to my remembrance. The joy and freedom that repentance brings is unspeakable. It changes how we see God, others and even ourselves. It brings our focus on God and not on self in pity for our situation.

When I first met with Janet and Peter I was operating in the spirits of deception, abandonment, control and fear. Through the leading of the Holy Spirit in our ministry times together we were able to discover the roots associated with each of these spirits and where their entrance points began. Through prayer and repentance these spirits were cast out of me. As I was delivered and set free I felt their oppressive weight lift off of me. My soul and my spirit became light as a feather inside of me. Then came the Holy Spirit.

After spending several weeks in daily repentance of my sins I headed out for an afternoon walk. I was enjoying listening to some praise music on my iPhone when I began to cross a bridge near our home. As soon as I stepped onto the wooden planks the Holy Spirit came upon me in such power that I needed to grab a hold of the cable railing beside me to keep from falling down. The Holy Spirit began to fill my heart with the sweetest love I have ever known. I was absolutely overflowing with the

Father's love as I staggered across the bridge and back, like a drunkard. Since that day's overwhelming encounter with the Holy Spirit He has met me in similar, but smaller ways, each day. Through these intimate times the Holy Spirit began drawing me to Him and filling me with the glory of the Lord; especially, during times of prayer or praise.

About a week later I was eating dinner out with two friends, an older couple that have been married for 30 years. As we talked, the conversation turned into an argument between this couple that could have been me with my wife weeks prior. I suddenly saw who I was as I was influenced by that same spirit. This was me before I went through healing. I was overcome with what this husband was still blinded with. It all became very real to me that moment. My heart cried out in compassion for this man. I quickly reminded him that his wife was God's daughter and God loves her.

But he continued to go on, speaking loudly out of his anger; stories that began to reveal the controlling spirit operating in his life. Before the evening was over I confronted my friend on his anger and control problems, argued against all of the lies he spoke out with the truth that had set me free from the same lies. I defended the honor of his wife who was trapped in the same abusive cycle in her marriage that caused my wife to leave me just two months earlier. I could speak out of freedom as truth has set me free.

As the enemy lost his grip on me I asked Janet how I could pray for my wife. She said by "standing in the gap." She wrote out a prayer for me to follow. I prayed it all the way home. The very next evening I spoke with my wife by phone and for the first time since our separation, I felt, this is my wife back.

Living in bondage to the enemy is like giving him open permission to steal, kill and destroy everything that matters to us and to our loved ones. That bondage manifested in my life as unhealthy control of our finances, making decisions based out of fear and not faith, uncontrolled outbursts of anger, irrational thinking, anxiety, deep depression, a critical spirit, living in pride, a sharp increase in selfishness, trying to control others, walking in offence and unforgiveness, justifying all of my decisions instead of taking the time to consider carefully the thoughts and feelings of my wife and children.

The Lord has used Janet and Peter to lead me through "Healing of the Heart" ministry, through which God has brought deliverance from the bondage and strongholds of the enemy in my life. They are faithful to the leading of the Holy Spirit and I am living proof.

Finally, by confessing the Word of God in my times of prayer, the Holy Spirit has been restoring my mind. He is continually correcting the wrong beliefs and lies, which I have picked up over my lifetime. My fears have been replaced with faith, my worries with hope, and I am continually being filled with the love of God for me on my journey with Him.

Peter Williams

Testimony from Dean

My life was filled with incredible loneliness and hatred most of my growing up years. I felt no one cared about me and love was completely absent in my life. Life was empty and full of confusion.

My mother was a Godly woman who spoke a word of life to me as a child saying, "you will be a man of God." This confused me as I had no sense of direction as my father taught me to steal, cheat and take revenge. My surroundings were lying and cheating so it seemed the natural thing to do. My life became so lonely I wanted to die. I thought I would take it in my own hands and filled my palm with pills one day to end it all, but stopped and wondered if God was real. I was completely at the end of my rope in loneliness and devastation beyond words, when something beautiful happened to me.

My lovely Lord brought me into His fold from darkness to light in 15 seconds. As I cried out to Him for mercy, I felt His compassion come upon me as He heard my desperate cry. That moment I felt the Holy Spirit fill me and I felt I was a new creation in Christ Jesus. I knew my old desires had passed away and I was now full of the love of God.

Soon after I became part of a cell group in our church that was lead by Peter and Janet Van Hierden. They came around me to disciple me. Our church is a group of 700 people so cell groups are a way of going to new levels. I had many health issues in my life; It is truly a miracle that I am still living today. My legs became an issue and the doctor gave me warning that if they could not be fixed, they would soon have to be amputated. This was to be a prayer request at the next gathering. I planned to go, but the last minute I could not, so I texted Janet to let her know. Her response was, "we will pray for you anyway." Three days later I felt heat starting at my waist and going down my legs and out my toes. I immediately went to the doctor and he said my legs were fine. I was so delighted I jumped up my five steps to my front door.

Three months later, some pain began to come back. The cell group came around me and collectively the revelation was that, "I had opened the door to the enemy and he had a right in my life." I knew what door had been opened and I repented and confessed to the Lord. I asked that each door be closed. My healing came back. I had been living in the manifest presence of God in a miraculous way since my salvation up until that point, but the presence seemed to leave me at that point. This became a heavy weight on me. I so desired His presence more than anything in the world.

Feeling sad and bewildered as to what may be happening I came back to cell group one evening. My pain seemed to be trying to return again in a small way. This time the message came as to "the power of suffering" as Janet writes in her book. She explained how to suffer with repentance, keeping our eyes completely on Jesus and not on self. I pondered this that evening and through the night. The next day the presence of God returned to me three times stronger than before. I was so excited to be walking in His manifest presence again, I knew what the "joy of the Lord is our strength" meant. I had to phone Janet to tell her the power of her message. I am again walking without any physical pain. I feel God is a wonder working God and He has me on a journey of knowing Him in depths that I could never fathom. I delight in knowing that the body of Christ is precious to me now and I no longer fear what man can do to me. I love people when before I did not want people in my life at all. I truly want to thank God and those that have come around me to help and teach me.

Dean Koopman

Conclusion

The heavenly Bridegroom wants to express His unconditional love for us. We must learn to hide in the shadow of His wing if we want to experience a deeper relationship with Jesus Christ. Time in His presence causes us to become so satisfied and refreshed that all other loves pale in comparison.

God invites us to Himself. "My lover spoke and said to me, 'Arise, my darling, my beautiful one, and come with me . . .'" He longs to be pursued as His Bride; passionate pursuit of our lover is our continual desire.

The final fruit of our relationship with Christ is the completion of the Great Commission, a united partnership between the Lord and His Bride. The Spirit and the Bride say, 'Come! (Rev. 22:17). The time has come for the Bride to understand her calling:

> Let us rejoice and be glad and give him glory! For the wedding of the Lamb has come, and his bride has made herself ready. Fine linen, bright and clean, was given her to wear. (Fine linen stands for the righteous acts of the saints). (Rev. 19:7–8)

I pray that you have been awakened to God's great pursuit over you, and you will pursue Him with passion!

CPSIA information can be obtained at www.ICGtesting.com
Printed in the USA
LVOW06s0304130214

373442LV00003B/4/P